ss.9/LEE

Good Grief

Carol Lee was educated in England, Wales, Africa and Egypt. She began her career in journalism on the *South Wales Echo* in Cardiff, and has since contributed to many of Britain's leading newspapers and magazines. She has been an 'agony aunt', a columnist on the *Daily Mail*, a feature writer on the *Daily Mirror* and a contributor to the *Observer*, the *Guardian*, the *Sunday Times*, *Cosmopolitan* and *Good Housekeeping*.

She also worked in television for four years, contributing to a number of major programmes. Her first play, *Feet First*, was performed at the King's Head Theatre in London. *Good Grief* is her fifth book.

UNIVERSITY OF EVANSVILLE
HARLAXTON COLLEGE LIBRARY
HARLAXTON MANOR
GRANTHAM LINCS

Also by Carol Lee

The Ostrich Position
Friday's Child
The Blind Side of Eden
Talking Tough

Good Grief

Experiencing Loss

Carol Lee

UNIVERSITY OF EVANSVILLE
HARLAXTON COLLEGE LIBRARY
HARLAXTON MANOR
GRANTHAM, LINCS.

FOURTH ESTATE · *London*

First published in Great Britain in 1994 by
Fourth Estate Limited
289 Westbourne Grove
London W11 2QA

Copyright © 1994 by Carol Lee

The right of Carol Lee to be identified as the author of
this work has been asserted by her in accordance with the
Copyright, Designs and Patents Act 1988.

A catalogue record for this book is available from the
British Library.

ISBN 1–85702–184–3

All rights reserved. No part of this publication may be
reproduced, transmitted, or stored in a retrieval system, in
any form or by any means, without permission in writing from
Fourth Estate Limited.

Typeset by York House Typographic Ltd
Printed in Great Britain by Biddles Ltd, Guildford and King's Lynn

For our Linda

Give sorrow words; the grief that does not speak
Whispers the o'er-fraught heart, and bids it break.

MACBETH

Contents

Acknowledgements

I would like to thank all the people who agreed to be interviewed and who generously gave their time and their stories.

Author's Note

Where necessary, people have been given different names, or initials, to protect their own identities and those of people close to them.

Foreword

The purpose of this book is to widen the scope of our understanding of the nature and experience of grief, and of the ways people cope with or react to it. For while grief, like love, is one of life's most profound experiences, it is also one of its most neglected.

Although many of us sense that denying grief can have bad consequences, a description of what it is to allow grief, and how this varies – and is similar – from person to person, is difficult to find. The notion seems to be that grief is separate from ordinary life, that it is something we suffer, like an illness, and then leave behind.

This is not borne out by people's experiences. Neither is the idea that loss or grief is something feeble, and that experiencing it is a sign of weakness. Many, if not most, of the feelings involved in the process of grieving would test the emotional equivalent of an athlete in Olympic condition. There is often, for example, within individual losses, a concern with moral issues arising out of these emotions. A sense of outrage is embedded in the grieving process, emerging, especially with the deaths of children, as a need for justice. Our sense of rightness about life is deeply offended when a child dies, and we often seek, in our grieving, to set this straight.

Many unexpected things were revealed in the course of interviewing for this book – one woman's wish for her grief not to end, another's fear of her dead father and another's need to smell a dead lover's clothes. There were many 'expected' things too – like the fact that coping with loss is often more difficult than imagination would ever admit and, therefore, all the more important to investigate.

I have thought of this book as an investigation, not because I am insensitive to the scores of people who appear within its pages, but the opposite. For my wish is not only to tell the stories, but to find out what they might possibly mean to all of us. If people can 'go through hell' and be standing at a bus-stop a month or a year later, chatting normally, how do they do it?

In essence, this book is concerned with people's journeys. A big part of the travelling we do in and through grief is what I have called the journey from the inside out. How do we negotiate this? How do people manage to cross the huge gulf between the powerful inner feelings which grief produces and an outside world which is impervious to their inner turmoil? How do people make the return journey out into the world again after suffering a tremendous blow? The world does not stop for an individual grief, yet with some griefs it can feel, from the inside, as if it has. How do people 'start it up' again? What helps them in this? What hinders them?

There can, in fact, be a hierarchy of grieving, in which the death of a friend, for instance, holds a lowly position, especially in the eyes, and balance sheets, of employers. If a close friend has died, a sympathetic employer might allow a half-day for the funeral. Many would not. As a personnel manager says: 'With compassionate leave we watch very carefully what it's for, otherwise people can take terrible liberties. I wouldn't expect to give someone compassionate leave if a friend had died . . . '

There is only so much room for grief, it seems. We cannot accept all deaths as our own grieving. We would go mad if we did. Yet all pain is linked. It does not occur in a vacuum, and new pains affect old wounds that we carry. How much loss can we be compassionate about?

This book explores many avenues, asking people what grief feels like looking back over their shoulders at it from a distance of five, ten or even twenty years. What did it mean then? Is it still important? Some people spoke of there being links between different griefs, one recalling another. *Good Grief* also poses many questions. What happens to older people when, to quote a woman in her seventies, their 'contracts are more with the dead than the living'? Is there a danger of becoming crazed or going mad through grieving?

In this respect there is something that I call 'general' grief, of which we all carry a little from our ordinary childhood losses, such as loss of innocence. There is a way in which all of us carry some grief, even if we have never lost anyone. In the same way as we carry some love, even if we have not loved deeply, so we carry some 'general' grief which is part of our humanness and compassion and which is connected to our personal griefs. There is the obvious example of 'national' or 'communal' grief which many of us experience after a tragedy where large numbers of people are killed, or when we hear of the murder of a child.

This book will show that our personal childhood griefs, where they are recognised by us, prepare us for our inevitable adult losses, like the loss of our parents. In other words, we do not have to come to our first adult grief completely unprepared.

It is obvious that the 'range' of grief, its intensity and duration vary according to one's personality. Some people, for instance, have very passionate griefs. Others have gentler ones. The basic conundrum to emerge from research is that there is no laid-down 'order' for grieving. It used to be considered that there were 'set stages', whereby people went through disbelief, then denial, then guilt and anger, and, finally, acceptance and resolution.

This is not thought to be the case any more. The people who have begun to realise this – bereavement counsellors and psychotherapists – say how valuable it would be for people to know this. For while grief has recognisable stages, even including one called 'hunting' (which is where some people search in crowds of shoppers and in cinemas for the face of a loved one who has died), these are also very individual. It is important for us to know that the way we accept or experience grief has much in common with others, but also says a great deal about ourselves and our relationships.

Following on from this, there are the habits and customs of grieving. The question of whether or not we view the body of someone who has died perplexed many of the people interviewed. Some felt cheated because they had not done so, some traumatised because they had. They very much wanted to know what others who had suffered bereavement had to say about this, for they felt isolated and ill informed when making a decision of this kind. Others were alienated by clichés. Comments like 'time will heal' and 'you're young, you'll get over it' added insult to injury in their eyes.

What those of us who are not suffering grief do to those who are is another important strand in this book. We have tendencies which we barely recognise, among them a tendency to take over people who are grieving. When putting an arm round someone to comfort them, we sometimes go further than that and try to control them, something I call 'infantilising'. We seem to do this most often when adults cry, as if an adult in tears breaks a number of conventions.

There is, I think, a strong argument for 'necessary tears', and our acceptance of them, but they bring up questions about the boundaries of grief. What are the boundaries between public and private emotions? What are the boundaries in ourselves between our capable adult personae and the hurt, wounded feelings which grief evokes in us, making some of us feel frighteningly like children again?

Implicit within these pages are questions – and answers – about loss of all kinds, especially those that are not usually written about. In talking about important losses, about grief and about recovering from grief, many people I interviewed expressed the wish that grief be allowed out of the closet, and be treated honestly. They were tired of it being taboo.

People were especially tired of the prejudice that grief takes up time which would be better spent on other things. Many people said that coming to terms with or recovering from a loss took more time than they ever imagined. They also described how grief is the guardian of a certain amount of time we otherwise spend extremely badly. It presents us with important opportunities for learning.

In accumulating the material for a book of this kind it has been necessary to interview a number of people across a wide range of experience. In acknowledging my debt to all the people who agreed to see me, I would like to say a little about how people were found, and how interviews were conducted. To begin with the latter, people were guaranteed anonymity. This was to protect individuals at a time when many were vulnerable, and also to protect family or friends. The same was true for professionals; bereavement counsellors or psychotherapists are not named so that the identity of the individuals who use their services is also safeguarded.

In the course of research I interviewed between 120 and 130 people in different parts of Britain. Professionals were approached through their various organisations, and individuals were 'found' in a variety of ways: some through bodies like schools, college and workplaces, some through self-help groups and some by word of mouth. I am especially indebted to people who, once they had been interviewed, took upon themselves the responsibility of phoning other people they knew to suggest they contact me.

While the bulk of this book is concerned with people's individual losses, a part of it involves looking at grief's causes in a broader context, which is where I believe they belong. There is, in any case, an exploration of *different* causes of loss: the difference, for example, between feelings which attend the loss of a loved one through a parting like divorce and those which follow a death.

Finally, I have been led by the research for this book to think of loss and grief as having a profoundly creative aspect, so that many – though not all – of us become 'bigger' rather than 'smaller' people as a result. One woman in her thirties says she has benefited from the death of a close childhood friend: 'Sometimes I have such a sharp sense of gratitude for being alive, it almost cuts me, as if life itself is sharp. I have this searing sense of aliveness, of being awake rather than dead.'

This book is essentially an affirmation, especially in a busy world, of the potential value of individual grief. It is also a portrait of what we share, of what we have in common.

* * *

CHAPTER 1

The Case for the Defence

The need we have to defend ourselves against loss, especially the loss of a partner

Our first instinct in the face of severe loss is to defend ourselves against the pain of it. This defence can take many forms, like keeping frantically busy. The process of defence against grief is especially strong with the loss of a partner, for this is the most intimate of losses. It is also the most 'comprehensive', since so much of our lives is rolled up in one person. In losing a partner we often lose a friend, a lover, a support and someone whom we can still, to some extent, be parented by. A partner can look after us when we are ill or distressed and becomes, as we grow older, the person who retains so much of our history. One woman described her husband as having been 'the witness' of her life's days, and said she felt 'wiped off the human map' in the months following his death.

With the loss of a partner we can thus feel a sense of being temporarily obliterated, and we seek ways of keeping this, and other painful feelings, at bay until we can cope with them. But in defending ourselves against the pain of loss we very often resort to strategies that also prevent us from getting comfort.

A woman in her mid-thirties says she surrounded herself with a layer of fat after a long-term relationship ended. This was a way of protecting herself from the possibility of another relationship, and more hurt. She gained a stone and a half in weight almost immediately, and then a further two stone in the year following. 'I was supposedly "comfort eating" to make up for what I'd lost, but it kept comfort away from me. It was a way of trying to make sure no man would look at me, and then no one else would hurt me. It was my way of hiding my hurt.

'I laughed and joked about the weight, and the more weight I gained, the more "jolly" I became and the more my hurt was hidden. Inside that big person there was a very wounded one, and all the extra fat stopped other people from seeing that. It was years before I faced up to how inconsolable I had become.'

Some people spoke of having a feeling of complete hopelessness straight after a death or a separation. Nothing in the world would 'do', nothing in the world would suffice or make them feel better, except having the person they had lost back again. One of grief's awful ironies is that, with the loss of a partner, the person who has died or left is the person who could offer most comfort. He or she is the person one is closest to, and who knows best one's secret and fallible self. At a time when this secret and fallible self most needs consolation and help, the person who has usually given this has gone.

This caused a woman of twenty-nine to feel invisible for a while after the sudden death of her husband in the third year of their marriage. So much of her tender, intimate and secret self had gone with him when he died that for a time she felt almost like a ghost: 'We had had a wonderful holiday a few months before he went, a second honeymoon, and he told me I would always be beautiful in his eyes, and that he had never for one instant regretted we were married. I felt so close to him throughout that holiday that it seemed as if we saw the world through one pair of eyes, not two. We were very much in harmony, and I know I was lucky to have that. But when he died, so suddenly [of a brain haemorrhage], I felt as if I had vanished as well as him, or at least as if the lovely parts of me had.'

For a year or two after her husband's death she viewed their closeness as a kind of penalty she was now having to pay for, 'as if you're not supposed to have something that good'. She also says: 'The feeling of almost invisibility wouldn't go away for a while. The nearest I can come to describing it is that when his eyes closed, something of me closed down too. A vision of me vanished, because no one else saw me as he did. To anyone else I wasn't beautiful. I was just an ordinary woman.'

People often liken the loss of a partner to 'losing a limb', showing how, in intimate relationships, the death or departure of one person deeply affects the 'wholeness' of the other. Whether it is through lack of appreciation or through the missing of eating a meal with someone, there can be a tremendous feeling of amputation.

The experience is so overwhelming for some that it can bring with it fears of total disintegration, and even of madness. It tests any notion we have of being capable, of being in control, of being adult. For the loss of a long-term partner, of a lover, a husband, a wife, takes away so much – and in some cases practically all – of the construction that has gone into the building of what a life looks like and has indeed become.

The props, the foundations, the windows, the safe roof all cave in with some deaths. And the hearth too goes dead. In many relationships, where someone is left on her or his own after fifteen – or fifty – years of being used to the close company of another person, the short-term reality of being without that person is, quite simply, shocking. Losing the safety of a secure relationship with the protection that brings felt for one person like 'a large crater' opening up: 'One minute you're going about your business as normal. The next, it's as if there's been an earthquake. Certainly that's what it felt like *emotionally*. In the weeks after my husband died I went from being an ordinary, capable person to almost a wreck. It was frightening how quickly it happened. One minute it seemed I was at the stove cooking a meal and the next I was standing in the kitchen wringing my hands. I seemed to be incapable of doing the simplest thing. I felt as if my abilities had vanished. The kitchen had been almost my second home for thirty years, and I was standing in it like a stranger.'

The need to defend oneself against experiences like these can be pronounced for some people. It is, after all, frightening suddenly to lose one's capabilities, especially for people who place a high value on these skills. Many so-called high achievers have a stronger wish to defend themselves than people who are more used to accepting their own vulnerability.

One such person is a man in his early fifties. In discussing his feelings about the death of his wife six years ago when she was in her mid-forties, he likened the experience to defending himself in a boxing-ring. It was an unusual ring, though, one where there was only one 'contender' – and no referee. The 'contender' was himself, and he was being hit, slapped around the ring on to the ropes. If he bounced back with his fists raised, he was hit again.

This was the nearest he could get to a description of what he felt for the first few weeks, and even months, after his wife died: 'I felt as if I had been punched, hit practically senseless. I was reeling from body blows and from physical pain. The actual physical pain of losing her was practically unbearable.'

A woman says of her battle with the physical pain of grief: 'It was like being stabbed, time and time again. Just when you dared to draw breath, to imagine you were *allowed* to breathe normally at last, it would hit again, this stabbing. The feeling I had was wanting to retreat from it, to defend myself. But how?'

The effect of the loss of someone as central to our lives as a partner can be severe. The shape of our lives has been threatened, and has been altered in a physical way. This, in turn, is felt in a physical way. One of the common words used for grief is that it 'hits' you. One of the common experiences people described as part of being 'hit' by grief was the sensation of physical pain. This was followed by a feeling of being rendered defenceless in the face of it.

A man in his mid-twenties believes that men have more trouble grieving than women since they are less ready to cry and to face loss, and that they suffer an extra burden because of this. For him, it is like being in a coffin: 'A lot of people, a lot of men, live in coffins, all closed off, all by themselves. They don't know how to get out.' He thinks the way out is through expressing feelings, and that if men, especially, could do this they would 'leave their coffins behind'.

The 'coffins' any of us, male or female, erect around ourselves are usually defences against rejection. We are afraid people will not accept us as we truly are, so we hide. In other words, we protect ourselves from a world which can be careless of our vulnerabilities.

At a time of grief we shut ourselves in these 'coffins' as a defence against pain. What they do, ironically, is to keep us locked away from the prospect of comfort. If lived in for too long, they sometimes become worse than the grief we were trying to avoid, and the remedy becomes more damaging than the affliction.

This happened to a woman who found that she had surrounded herself with 'an invisible bubble'. Within about a week of her husband's leaving her for another woman she found this 'bubble', like an extra skin, was around her. It was something which no one else could see, but which she could not break or push her way out of: 'I was hearing things as if through a thick skin. I was surrounded by this skin, a few feet away from me, like being in a large, invisible balloon. It meant I couldn't feel properly – not anyone or anything outside me, that is – because nothing could get through this "skin". And I couldn't hear. Or at least I could, but as if people were speaking from a long way off in a muffled way. It was the same with the radio or the television.' She felt 'starved' by this experience, and quite hopeless, for although she saw people, she could not 'connect' with them, and sometimes going out only added to her misery.

She then began to realise that she had caused 'the bubble' herself, and that she had created it as a defence against her anger. She discovered that she was furious at being left, as well as extremely upset, and while she knew how to cope with being upset by crying, she did not know how to cope with the anger. So she defended herself against it by placing herself out of reach of further hurt. 'I felt the skin had been put round me by someone or something else, some malign force. It wasn't. I did it myself. I had been badly hurt, and I didn't realise how angry I was about this. I surrounded myself with a protective layer because I didn't want more hurt, but the protection stopped me getting comfort.'

A severe loss, especially in the case of a death, hits us hard. Whether we have loved the person deeply or not, what we have done with the years and who we have become through living them have been fashioned by those whom we have cared for, and especially whom we have lived with.

Even with the loss of someone who is not very close we are still accustomed to their being there as part of what a psychoanalyst called 'the stage-set' of our lives. They make up the full scenery of how we view our world. If they live on different continents, or are rarely seen, they have a place in our lives all the same and form part of our all-important personal history. Using the analogy of a stage-set, the removal of even a small prop in this edifice can make us feel unsafe. If, as often happens with grief, a number of 'props' are removed at the same time, then this feeling of insecurity can become quite threatening. Perhaps the whole world – in other words, our own personal stage – is going to collapse completely. Perhaps nothing is safe.

The sense that our personally constructed world of relationships and security is being threatened makes us defensive within grief as well as aggressive, or angry. It does not, after all, seem 'fair' or 'just' that we should build relationships to have them knocked down.

A woman in her mid-forties reported having strong resentment and anger for quite some time after the death of a male friend slightly younger than herself. She felt a kind of bitterness after his death that she did not experience after her father's death eighteen months later. She was much closer to her father than she was to her friend, but her father's death was 'easier', for it made her sad, not angry. Her friend's death she railed against, and found she was so disturbed by it that she had to leave the gathering after his funeral to go and cry by herself: 'I wanted to lick my wounds in private. My emotions were very confused, but basically I felt he was too young to die. There was so much left for him to do, so much life to enjoy. Something wasn't fair about his death, and I couldn't be settled about it for quite a while. I just sat on the station by myself on the way home and just cried and cried and cried till the train came.'

Another woman who lost a male friend had an angry, disturbing dream a few nights after his death. In the dream her friend was still alive, but dreadfully thin, almost skeletal, from his long illness. She says: 'I was cruelly shaking him, trying to force him back towards life again. I was very disturbed when I woke up, by my cruelty, for he was so ill in the dream I should have left him in peace. I afterwards realised it was my anger coming out. We had been close, and I didn't want him to leave me.'

Being angry with people who have died is not an unusual method of defence if they are our partners, and therefore the recipients of so much of our intimate and secret selves. A man whose wife died after they had been married for twenty-eight years found that the emotions thrown up by loss played tricks, even with the love he and his wife had felt for each other. They had had a good marriage, and he would have said, before his wife died, that they were both sure of this, and of their love.

They had developed careers at different stages in their lives, the one helping the other when needed, and since his wife had been ill for some time, they had also, in the final months of her illness, had time to go over their love together, to talk through their lives. Despite all this, despite the husband's vigil at his wife's bedside and twenty-eight good years, within a week of his wife's death this husband had decided she had not loved him after all. 'I rang up someone close to us who had also visited her and said: "Did she say anything about me behind my back? Did she say anything she never told me?" And the woman I asked was most surprised because she could never have believed I would have done that. Basically I had this strong feeling, all of a sudden, that she [his wife] didn't love me, because if she loved me, then she wouldn't have died. She wouldn't have left me with all the pain of losing her.'

To someone who has never suffered a severe loss it may seem difficult to imagine that the forces of grieving can be so powerful as to wipe out, for a while, the reality of twenty-eight years of commitment. The fact that this can and does happen, though usually only temporarily, shows how powerful the emotions involved in grieving can be.

They produce defences which, in the short term, can make us put up our fists to fight off the pain. We pretend that a wife does not love us. The defence works, sometimes only for seconds or minutes, before the next stab of truth cuts through it. But at least it has been a short break, a small rest, from painful reality.

The full extent of this reality can be difficult to take in all at once, for not only does it hurt or grieve us when someone dies, but it also crosses our will, and fundamentally thwarts us. Our will, or our deepest wish, is to have the person back again. But in this we are absolutely denied what we long for. We experience for a short time a wish for the impossible, an almost overpowering need to have what cannot be, the dead or departed person back. We want life to be exactly as it was before this awful thing happened. But we cannot have what we want. Despite our wish not to be deprived of the person we love, despite all our yearnings, nothing can be changed. She or he has gone – and that is that.

As adults this leaves us in the almost unbelievable position where something major has occurred in our personal lives without a word or gesture of consultation. We are not, other than in exceptional circumstances, consulted about the death of someone close to us. It just happens. It takes someone away from us, and gives us no choice whatsoever in their leaving. In sudden deaths, people just vanish. They were here one moment saying yes, they will get the car fixed in the morning, or bring round a CD they want us to hear . . . and those are the last words they say to us.

A woman who lost her father when she was in her late thirties remembers the feeling of impotence his death evoked in her. She could not believe for a while that there was not a single thing she could do about it: 'I've always been used to action, and to plans of action. At work if things haven't been going right, I have cleared the desk and worked out a plan for what needs to happen. In the end it doesn't matter if the plan is carried out or not because what matters is making it – and feeling you have the power to make it.

'That was what struck me after my father's death. There was nothing, nothing at all I could do about it, and I think that feeling caused me grief on top of the grief I was already feeling. It was the first time in my life I couldn't escape. There was no plan in my mind I could use to get out of this, and I didn't like that feeling. Mind you, I had to learn to accept it. Besides missing my dad, it was probably the hardest thing I had to do.'

While a roof falling in makes us feel unsafe, being heavily thwarted can enrage us. Our defensiveness comes into play as a way of protecting ourselves, both from the insecurity and from the anger at being thwarted. We have learned to cope with ordinary thwarting or frustration of our wishes, but we also depend on there being a balance in order to survive – a certain amount of success and achievement. We build careers, relationships, reputations around this balance, and all this becomes intricately woven, making up the sum total of who we are. In removing from us someone we love – or even someone we do not love, but have become accustomed to – one of the main strands of our life disappears.

This presents us, oddly enough, with failure as well as loss. It takes from us someone we have an investment in, someone we have spent time with, and whom we have involved in our energy and emotions. In the case of a death, not only is someone taken away from us against our wishes, but we are left devoid of the usual potency of our skills and bargaining powers. Death is the one thing about life that no amount of hard work, pleading, conniving, juggling or paying the piper can alter: it is impervious and irrevocable.

It is not surprising, therefore, that the experience of grief after a large loss can toughen people up, though it can also, of course, do the opposite. Five years after his wife's death one widower says: 'I have this mental image of soldiers coming back from a war, and I think grief either crushes you or makes you stronger.' He explains that which effect it has depends on whether people accept grief, or grieve badly. He defines grieving badly as refusing to accept grief or turning your back on it: 'Grief does set you apart. People who have gone through it are different. That's one of the things you have to accept. And people who don't want to accept that, who want to stay the same as they were before, get beaten by it. People who try to suppress it, I think it crushes them eventually and makes them timid.'

The image of war, and of people who grieve as being soldiers returning battle-scarred from an emotional front line, is illuminating. For one of the problems with grief is that it is often viewed as a backwater, where mourners sit around and cry a good deal and do very little. Some people see grief and giving in to it as weak. In reality many of the emotions surrounding a severe loss are, in fact, 'hard' or angry ones, and make a mockery of the idea that to give in to grief is a failing.

Looking at the way loss thwarts us, or crosses our will, and at the way grief can make us into battling soldiers, what would be inappropriate would be to behave as if nothing had happened. What would be equally out of place would be not to try, in some small way, to defend ourselves against the 'enemy'. It would indeed be peculiar to have little reaction when a person we love, someone who may have been by our side for many years, is physically removed – for good. In the case of an untimely death it would seem unbelievable if powerful emotions were not a part of the grieving experience. Someone we love, need and have become used to is removed from our lives; and in terms of our life's needs, habits and treasured hopes, that takes a large amount of adjusting to. Within this adjustment there is the business of coming to terms with what has happened, and then slowly filling in, moving away from or replacing a large 'black hole'.

In the case of a sudden loss our emotions are roaming around, pulling at us, tugging us. They can easily, for a short time, turn themselves into so many angry, phantom children demanding to be listened to all at once. At its most severe (and not all grief is severe), it can be difficult to withstand this emotional buffeting which varies from the most abject despair to towering rage, from a feeling of being almost completely impotent to a driving fury which is just as painful because it has no target. Where do you take it? What do you do with it? And, in any case, are you in charge of it, or is it in charge of you?

A woman in her early thirties who lost the man she lived with in a motor-cycle accident ten years ago still clearly remembers being in the grip of very powerful emotions following his death. She also remembers the antidote, or the defence, she used against her considerable anger: she spent hours and hours chopping wood. She described this demanding physical activity as a way of assuaging her feelings and of diverting the 'bad behaviour' which she suffered from during her grieving: 'I began to become irritated, frustrated and angry with people around me for very small, petty things. I think in retrospect it's all part of the anger which you do experience, especially from an abrupt, unexpected loss. I was getting aggravated with people for reasons which logically I knew weren't on, but it didn't stop me feeling the things I did. I knew the problem was within me, that it wasn't other people's fault, but it didn't help much at the time knowing that.

'Luckily I live in the country and in a place where we had an open fire. So I chopped wood. I can thoroughly recommend it. It got rid of my anger and aggression and stopped me barking at people who really didn't deserve my bad temper.'

The further aspect of grief for a partner that makes it difficult to bear, and makes us defensive in the face of it, is the number of roles lost within one person, and the variety of functions. We can lose in a husband or wife an administrator, a gardener, a provider, a lover, a parent for our children and the only person in the world who understands our jokes or who recognises our beauty. These different roles were discussed by a senior social worker who is employed full-time at a large teaching hospice. She linked them to the way in which grief can crush someone and make them timid.

In speaking of grief generally she had named the main needs of the bereaved people who came to her as being to be allowed to talk and to be given time and permission to grieve in their own way. When asked, aside from these, what would be most helpful to people in grief, she gave a surprising answer: 'A gift of £5,000.' This money would help people to be able to afford to look after themselves, and to 'buy in' for a short time the roles they had lost in the person who had died. 'A lot of the bereaved I see would be substantially helped by the gift of £5,000. I know that's an unfashionable thing to say, but it would support their independence at a time when they've lost so much. It would mean, for example, that they could use cars to go to places to arrange all the things they have to when they're still in a state of shock. It would mean that all the roles that are now left unfilled since the person died could at least be mitigated for a while.'

She explained that many of the women and men who had lost long-term partners found themselves having to do things they were not used to. Some of these things they had never done before, and could not begin to learn to do, at least not immediately. If the person who died was the one who drove the car, for example, the person left might have to get around on buses at a time when they were most vulnerable. If the person who died did all the cooking, or shopping, then the person left would find himself or herself confronted with an essential task which, though relatively simple, felt strange and frightening.

The social worker continued: 'Especially for older people, when someone dies there are all manner of things *they* used to do that the person left behind now has to do on his or her own. And many people, particularly in the early stages of grief, get very anxious about this. If money were available, a lot of this anxiety could be taken away – or at least reduced. You could afford to pay somebody £5 to cut the hedge or do the garden. You wouldn't have to worry about finding out how to get to the coroner's office . . . you could afford to have a car to the cemetery. In the months following a death you could afford to go to the cemetery when you needed to without worrying if you could make the journey or afford the fare.

'For poor people £5,000 would be something for their independence, or even for their self-esteem, for their power. For they've lost power. They've lost a breadwinner or a cook or a household manager, and they've lost status. If the breadwinner has gone, they've lost their ability to earn money, and they've lost so much. In the short term, until people are able to adjust, money would fill some of those gaps.'

A woman in her late seventies who has experienced the kind of problems this social worker outlined agreed that a shortage of money made her grieving harsher and much more difficult. She lives in the country and it is ten years since her husband died. She recalls standing in a florist's about a month after his death, wanting to buy some flowers to take to the grave. She had not bought flowers before, having come from a family where money was always in short supply. She chose what she wanted, and then found the price asked for the flowers was way beyond what she expected: 'I can't remember what it was now, but I'd only chosen a few. I felt my stomach turn over when she told me how much it would be. But I didn't want to say I wouldn't take them. I was too ashamed. So I bought them, and I cried in the bus on the way home, trying to keep my face to the window so no one would see me.' Laughing now, she says: 'I hated those flowers. I took them home, and I felt like throwing them away.'

She thinks it would help a good deal if people were given a small sum of money when their husband or wife died, something like an extra amount on their pension: 'If there's no money, you have to think about everything. Can you afford flowers? Can you afford shoes for the funeral or will the old ones do? And you don't want to invite people back to the house if you can't afford to make proper sandwiches for them. You start to feel mean, as if you're worrying about money when you should be worrying about death. And it makes you feel hard – and guilty.'

This feeling of guilt arises from a desire to honour the dead with what is best. Even though that cannot be properly expressed in financial terms, to have to be penny-pinching over funeral arrangements seems dishonourable. Like weddings, funerals are ceremonies where people wish to display love through making things beautiful.

But money itself can only be a salve for grief's smaller indignities. Grief's larger affronts we counter, initially, through defensive mechanisms. A psychotherapist described the process of defending oneself against hurt as something which we all do in some measure: 'Defences are necessary from time to time for all of us, and everyone has their own pace of tolerating more feeling. If for a while, after grief, someone is defended, that is not necessarily bad. It's knowing what's happening that matters. If you know you are defending yourself for a short time, and this is necessary, because of work, say, then you will begin to allow the time for grief to happen.

'I suppose flexible defences would be the best thing to have. If the defences are rigid, they can cause trouble. If they are flexible, then the person will find themselves able to tolerate more feeling, and move forward and back a little, like a wave.'

This acceptance of defence as a creative rather than a shutting-out mechanism enables grief to be slowly absorbed into the sum total of our lives. It stops it becoming the 'enemy within', an enemy which depletes our precious store of vitality and resilience as heavily as the 'coffins' or the bubble mentioned earlier. When we allow grief to become our enemy, we bring about defensive behaviour anyway.

Two of the commonest ways in which we defend ourselves against grief are by denying that the loss occurred and by deciding to delay the grieving process for another time. The former is usually a short-term strategy, an example of which was given by a home help who visits many elderly people as part of her job: 'For quite a few months sometimes they will just not accept the person has died. I visited one elderly lady who insisted on cooking all her meals for two for quite a while after her husband died. I think one part of her knew he had gone, but the other part just couldn't accept it. It was only when she saw how expensive it was getting that she stopped.'

Delay as a defence mechanism is far more prevalent. Behind it is the thought, I'll get on with life for now, put it behind me, and maybe if I'm lucky it will go away and I won't need to look at it. A man in his forties who had lost the woman he had lived with for three years six months before being interviewed says of his experience: 'I think I'm dipping a toe in and out of grief. I don't think I've had the courage yet to properly face it. Some mornings I feel fine and I think I can see my way forward. Then it hits me like a blow in the stomach, and I begin to realise what I've lost.

'I feel as if I'm having my grief in little bits and pieces. There's so much going on at work, and one of my sons by my first marriage is in a bit of trouble and needs my help. So I've got to be strong. But I know there's something I've got to go through – or at least I feel there is.'

About a month after his partner died he managed to get away for the day and ended up walking by the sea. 'I found I was trying not to get my shoes wet, and I thought, this is what I'm doing, I'm walking along the edge [of grief] when I should be jumping in.' He says that he needs 'time' to make the jump into the risky business of more fully accepting his loss, and concludes: 'The danger will be if I don't find – or make – it.'

There is a danger in avoiding the grieving process, for if we do not recognise our losses and express our griefs, they become like dead weights within us, dragging on our lives, keeping us down. The effect, therefore, of avoiding grief is the opposite of what is intended. Instead of leaving us free to walk along beaches, and get on with 'the good things in life', it keeps us back or retards us. It prevents the good things from happening deep down because there is something else in the way – a dead weight, 'an enemy within', a layer of fat or a deathly bubble.

* * *

CHAPTER 2

Wise Adults and Other Children

The way in which the loss of children affects us differently, and may often drive us to action

The death of a child is considered by doctors and psychologists to be the most painful grief we can suffer. One of the main reasons for this is that it affects our sense of 'rightness' and of balance in the world. In accepting death itself as inevitable, we cope, as adults, with the loss of someone who has had a long life. There is not much we need to do about it. With a young, untimely or premature death there is.

Perhaps this is why the loss of a child very often drives us towards action. Rather than defending ourselves by withdrawing into our sorrow, we seem to feel the need to 'come out' and do something, for the death of a child or a young adult offends us deeply. The child has been given no time to develop; we have been given no time to know her or him as an adult. What sense does that make of living, of life? Who or what brings this state of affairs about? Who was to blame for this?

The first thing we do is to ask the questions which accompany an untimely death, and to try to apportion blame through the answers. It is an attempt to find a culprit for what is the most unacceptable loss. And while questions of blame will arise from any premature parting, they are often particularly vociferous with a young death. The first target is usually oneself. We castigate ourselves with thoughts like, I should never have let him have the day off school, I shouldn't have made her catch an earlier train or if only I hadn't insisted he go to Scouts today, he would still be alive. In other words, we imagine the tragedy is our fault.

While seeking to blame by itself would be negative, its positive aspect is to keep our minds busy in a search for meaning, and for justice. This search can make parents who have lost small children, or have lost children as young adults in their teens or twenties, very 'capable'. It can make them develop skills, and it can make them behave in ways they never imagined. This is what happened to Shirley, who lost her eighteen-year-old son when the ship he was racing in sank in a storm off the coast of Bermuda. She found that within days of her son's death she was embarked on a course of action. She had not planned it, but almost instinctively the questions tumbling through her mind led her to try to get to the root of what exactly had happened to her son.

The first thing Shirley did was to meet the survivors of the tragedy, arranging through the Sail Training Association that they be flown to London: 'I just wanted to know things about the last weeks of his life. Did he eat fish on the boat? Because he didn't at home. Did he wash? Was he happy? They were all so young themselves, and some of them suffering dreadful exposure burns. My heart went out to them for what they'd been through. It was very healing to spend time with them. Some of us just fell into each other's arms, and we laughed and cried.'

Shirley did not, in the end, ask too many questions about what had actually happened because the survivors were themselves young, and some were still in a state of shock. Also, she feared knowing the worst – that her son had been swept away into shark-infested waters, or trapped. But her insistence on meeting these young people and their families set her on a path which took up the next three years of her life. It became obvious from the little that was said that there were discrepancies between the shipowner's version of events and the survivors'. Furthermore, she got the impression that the survivors had been told not to talk, either to their parents or to anyone else, about what had gone on.

This led her towards seeking a public inquiry into the accident in which eighteen people besides her son died. She found anger a useful companion, and while the inquiry did not give her the result she wanted, she does not regret the time spent on it. Shirley feels that she gained a great deal in her quest for answers, and for justice, and that no one can take that away from her. She has since been in touch with many other people who have lost children: 'What it's done for most of the people I know is it's made us very strong and invulnerable, because if somebody's actually taken away your only son and killed him there's almost nothing terrible they can ever do to you again. So when you're fighting for justice, or you're fighting to find out what happened, what can they do to you? They can't really do anything, so it makes you quite a dangerous enemy, because you have nothing to lose, and they do fear you.'

Whether, in the short term, the blame for the death of a child is turned inwards to oneself, or out on to other people – towards fate, or a god, or a shipowner – it is a common reaction. It can seem a very negative thing to do, but it is an essential part of a long process from impotence towards action. It is part of the work of reasserting our own control over an event by bringing our minds to bear on it. We can turn our turbulent emotions about something which so deeply affects us into protests about what we think of as 'just' or 'normal'.

Our minds tell us there has to be a cause, and if there is a cause, someone was responsible, and something can then be done. If a culprit can be found, that culprit can be punished, and perhaps the awful feeling that this is simply not right will go away. If someone is punished, maybe that will be the solution to a seemingly unremitting pain which one fears is never going to end.

A wish for either justice or punishment keeps the mind busy through a loss which feels unendurable because it so profoundly goes against our expectations of life. It is the mind's way of trying to negotiate itself, like a flimsy canoe, through torrents of emotions it is not used to. It is a way of trying to prevent that canoe from tipping over in the rapids. In other words, it is a way of trying to stop ourselves from 'going crazy'.

Our reactions in trying to 'right' this canoe demonstrate clearly that grief does not just involve us in emotions and actions which some call 'weak'. While tearfulness and feelings of impotence and despair attend all severe losses, so do other, powerful emotions. There are as many 'hard' emotions accompanying grief, ones like anger, and aggression, as there are 'soft' ones like sadness. Anger would seem, in any case, a reasonable response to losing something or someone we would dearly love to keep. This is especially so with children. The reason for this is that a child's death does many things to all of us.

It not only takes from parents someone they are still nurturing, but it also offends a general sense of justice those of us who are not the child's parents have about life, and about the reason for living. We accept that old people must die, and sad as it makes us to lose grandparents, mentors and wise adults in our lives, this does not usually make us distraught. The death of a child – the most untimely death – threatens a natural order whereby parents and older people are expected to die first, and thus makes us insecure and mindful of how random life can be. It reminds us that we are not as much in control of events as we would like to think.

A child's death threatens deep, instinctual necessities or codes that we are barely aware of, but which we value highly. Innocence is among the most prized of these. We think of children as being the keepers of innocence, even – or perhaps especially – in highly commercialised times. Advertisers are fully aware of the money-spinning potential of children's innocence, and use it where they can to promote their products. As well as exploiting their 'lovability' in TV advertisements, commerce uses children for its own ends by selling them endless sweets, with no regard for their health. Commercial values do not hold dear the natural wisdoms which emerge through childhood innocence, and in fact seek to pollute them by making consumers out of children.

We are, nevertheless, deeply attracted to innocence. Whether religious or not, it is part of our human faith that you do not betray the innocence of a child, and part of our own tragedy when we do. Without consciously realising it, we rely upon the innocence of children to rescue us from dark, cynical hours and to give us faith and hope.

Beauty, in its broadest sense, is something else which a child's death offends or undermines. For young children are physically appealing and lovable in a way that adults slowly lose as they get older. Children are, if you like, naturally beautiful, and when they are lost to us we pine for this beauty. Our innate sense of justice is another issue which a child's death calls into question. 'Can there possibly be a just god?' is a question often asked following the deaths of children. For children who die have not had time to live, to become adult. They have not been given a chance. More particularly, they have not been given a chance to form adult relationships of their own, and to have their own children.

There is in most of us a wish for people to be treated well. There is especially a wish for children to be treated well, which is one of the reasons why children are so important in helping us become compassionate. They are there to be taken care of, and while we might do that badly in many ways, and on many occasions, that is still their gift, that they give us the possibility for good care and the development, therefore, of compassion. Sadness and outrage arising from a wish for safety and justice are felt in some measure at the senseless deaths of all children. Children are important to us because of these feelings which they produce, and the opportunity they give us to experience them and to act on them as best we can.

A child's death also cuts into our confidence about the future. If there were no children at all to look forward to, there would be no human future. We do not need to have children of our own to feel this, or to lose a child of our own to know this is true. Children are imperative, or imperatives, to our futures. The death of one child can easily 'stop the future' for a while, or at least the prospect of it.

A combination of all of these – the symbolic losses of innocence, faith, beauty and hope, and our own wish to be compassionate – makes us fight to defend the rights of children more dearly than if these rights were our own. It is a terrible thing to have lost our past, as can happen when we lose a partner. It is an even more terrible fate to lose the prospect of our future.

This explains why people are often tenacious in their fight for justice when a child or a young person has died. It explains why they act to form charities and foundations in their children's names, as Shirley did. A couple who lost a daughter donated a bench in the school playground with her name on it. And a couple whose daughter was accidentally shot and killed while travelling through the Khyber Pass began a foundation for young artists in her name. They have also had T-shirts printed up with a picture of her face on them because they want at least an image of her to remain in their working lives.

The fact that the death of a young person results in the most questions and the most actions is not surprising. Part of the wish to 'do' something must be to dissipate some of the intense emotions sudden or young death produces. There is the need, for example, to 'get all the facts', and run through them time after time. This would happen in any sudden death, and is pronounced where a death is not only unexpected, but also involves someone young.

Bill spoke of this in recounting the lengths he went to in order to 'fill in the picture' of the last hours and days of his son's life. His son, who was seventeen, had been on holiday with American relatives, distant cousins, when he was hit by a car. Bill flew out to the USA, and did not come back for almost a month: 'I spoke to everybody. I spoke to the police, I went knocking on people's houses, I visited the hospital where his body was taken. I just needed people to tell me about him. I spent hours, days, standing on or near the spot where he was killed. I had to have those last pieces of his life with me before I could lay him to rest, and have any peace for myself.'

Fours years later Bill feels at peace, and does not regret what he did. 'I think a few people thought I'd taken leave of my senses, and maybe I had for a short while. But I loved that boy, and I wasn't going to let him go, I wasn't going to let him be buried until I'd finished what needed to be done.'

Another father, Eric, who lost his only daughter after his wife and he were divorced, recalls something not dissimilar. She too was killed in a car accident, when she was nineteen years old. He says: 'My wife phoned to tell me that Tess had been run over while visiting a friend. She was staying with her for the weekend, and had been knocked down and killed on a pedestrian crossing.'

Although the friend's home was 150 miles away from his ex-wife's, it was there that Eric headed for: 'I spent the best part of a week up there. The first place I went to after the hospital where her body had been taken was the crossing. I just stood there and watched the traffic going over it. I couldn't bring myself to walk over it. I just stood for hours and watched . . .'

Eric feels it was right to do this, that it was a vital part of his grieving to stand, until it got dark, watching traffic speed past the spot where his daughter had been killed: 'I still can't explain *why* I did it. It was a kind of instinct that I had to, and it was right. Eventually, when I'd seen enough cars go over the spot, I was ready to walk away, but wild horses wouldn't have dragged me away before that.'

Emotions at the loss of a young person can be especially difficult when a loss is not only sudden or untimely, but also malicious. This was the case with a couple whose daughter had been murdered, and who were featured on the BBC1 programme *Crime Limited* (2 September 1993). Part of their grieving hinged on anticipation that their daughter's killer would be brought to justice. While the killer was at large they felt their mourning could not be completed. This, however, changed after they met, through the BBC, a prisoner who was 'doing time' for murder. He was not, in the couple's mind, the 'usual picture of a murderer'. He was caring and thoughtful, and deeply regretted the crime he had committed.

They began to correspond, and the couple's empathy with the man increased. The prisoner eventually wrote to tell them that some of the men in prison with him had broken down and cried when he had read out their letters to him revealing their feelings about their loss. The couple were moved by this and, although they still felt the grief at the death of their daughter would 'never be finished', they were able to let go of some of their own pain.

In allowing themselves to be helped in this way the couple differed from another family described by a senior social worker. Their young daughter, aged seven or eight, had been killed by a woman motorist when the child ran out into the road. The motorist had stood little or no chance of avoiding the child, and was distraught at what had happened.

Police examination of skid-marks, car brakes, tyres and so on confirmed that the death was not the driver's fault, but the child's family could not accept this. They screamed abuse at her at the court hearing more than a year later when she was officially pronounced 'blameless'. Many years on, the car driver feels the incident will never leave her; her life has been ruined because she killed a child – however unintentionally.

It seems that this family was unwilling or unable to accept the crossing of their will. They could not allow themselves to be subject to the same ordinary events as the rest of us – accidents, losses, disappointments. In other words, they could not forgive life for being as it is, something not entirely devoted to their wishes. Because of this, the dead child's family have not been healed by the obvious distress and penitence shown by the car driver. Their insistence or revenge has, in turn, had its effect on the driver.

This is in contrast to a couple I interviewed whose seven-year-old son was killed on the road by a male car driver. Again, the child had run out, and the driver, a man in his fifties, was shocked to have been involved in his death. Three days after the accident he visited the child's family. Judith, the child's mother, says: 'We didn't know who he was at that point. The accident happened outside my mother-in-law's. We only knew from witnesses that it wasn't the driver's fault.' She was startled to find him at the door a few days later. He introduced himself, and explained he had come to say how sorry he was about what had happened and to ask if there was anything he could do to help. 'He was a really nice, quiet person, and he was obviously suffering. At one point, looking at him, my heart really went out to him. I know we'd lost a son, and that will never leave us, but I began to think what it was like from his point of view. It would stay in his mind, probably all his life.

'I was glad he came. I think it put a part of our minds at rest, and I think it helped him too.'

Alan too was involved in a road accident in which a child died. He was in his early thirties when his car struck and killed a boy of twelve who had run on to the road from behind a parked car. Fifteen years later he says: 'After not sleeping for days I went round to see the family. I didn't know what my reception would be, but anything was better than what I was going through, even insults.'

At the time he had no children of his own, but had recently married, and he and his wife were planning to begin a family: 'I wouldn't let her [his wife] come with me. She wanted to, but if anything awful did happen, I didn't want her to be a part of it. I was also warned my visit could have legal consequences, but you can't live your life like that, putting legal matters over human affairs.' In fact, the child's family welcomed him in. 'It was the best thing I did. We cried together. They had lost a young son, and I felt dreadful for that. They also understood how I felt. I think if I hadn't gone round, if I hadn't shared something with them, it would have been with me for ever. I would never have had peace from it.'

The ability to accept loss, and to forgive life, fate, God, oneself or the universe is crucial to justice. For if every one of us required blood for blood, an eye for an eye, and did not have the power for forgiveness and recovery, grief would go on without end. If we cannot or will not allow the tears of strangers to comfort us, then we will remain inconsolable.

The distinction between wanting justice and seeking revenge after the death of a young person is an important one to make, for it deeply affects our ability to recover from a loss, not just at a personal level, but at a general one too.

This was demonstrated through the death of Tim Parry, aged twelve, from an IRA bomb planted in Warrington. Within months of their son's death, Tim's parents, Colin and Wendy Parry, visited both Northern Ireland and the Irish Republic, talking to people, priests and politicians. Their mission was to use the loss of their son as a means of discussing 'the troubles' in Ireland. They wanted to ask the many people they saw why they were at war with each other, and why the war could not be ended. Was peace not an option? Why could it not be found? They were obviously driven by the need to do something that would bring good out of bad, as were the thousands of people from Northern Ireland and the Republic alike who wrote to them.

Since their visit Mr and Mrs Parry have been asked to write a book, which will be called *An Ordinary Boy*. When agreeing to do this, they said: 'We see the book as a story about what happens to a family when something unbelievable happens, and also as a commentary on the current situation in Ireland.'

All the people I spoke with who had lost children, even adult children in their twenties, showed a powerful desire to prevent others from suffering as they had done. They were, in other words, people who had used their suffering creatively, even though one mother described losing a child as being left with a stark choice: 'Life or annihilation.' For while the death of a child is the most terrible thing that can happen to a parent, it also produces needs in all of us to make things better, to strive to mitigate such a tragedy. The wish to do something following an untimely death – to sue, to create a foundation, to start a memorial fund – is strong. Partly it is a way of trying to ensure that a young life lives on.

People who lost children when they were small, or as young adults, showed a pronounced need to continue their children's lives. They kept faith through insisting on naming, or counting, their children after their deaths. This became apparent when people spoke of what they did when someone they met at a dinner party, or a bus-stop, asked them how many children they had. It was a question they came to dread, for many, initially, did not know what to do: to tell the truth was to risk opening a wound again; to tell a lie was to deny a life. The first time one man and his wife were asked at a dinner party how many children they had was only a few months after their son had died. The father says: 'I knew R. [his wife] couldn't answer. But I knew if I told the truth, if I said: "Well, we did have three children, but one died", I wouldn't get through the sentence. And I didn't want to upset the host and his wife either, who were close friends. So, in the end, I said: "Two." And as soon as I said it I knew what a mistake it was. I felt as if I had denied my son his life, and I said there and then I would never do it again.'

People who survive the untimely, sudden or violent deaths of those close to them, and who do this strongly and compassionately, not vengefully, are changed by the experience. It is as if they fully grow up and become their own parents, people who are able, as you would with a hurt child, to make their grief better, and to become bigger because of the experience rather than smaller. They have, as one person put it, 'more room in their hearts'.

For those who do this there is a definite gain in stature. Whether this is from having 'more room in their hearts', or from setting up public inquiries, or from simple acceptance of life's often random quality, a change takes place. In essence they assume more authority than they had before. This authority belongs firmly to them. It is as if they have 'earned' it, and because of it they are not easy to cross or to question.

They may previously have been people who looked to a higher authority, like a court of law or an institution, for their justice. They often end up looking to themselves. For if grief does not make them timid, it can make them strong.

Through interviewing people who have lost children it is possible to see how both the Buddhist and Christian religions have based much of their philosophy on worshipping a child. For the death of a child can transform people, and produce in them a wish and an impetus to act so that the child will not have died in vain. While the pain and the hurt of the death never completely vanish, the spontaneous affection and love which children so easily give and attract seem to live on in the parents. It especially lives on in their relationships with grandchildren, who become even more cherished and important.

People can become brave through losing children. Like the couple from Warrington they will try to balance loss with gain by seeking even wider issues than an individual tragedy to challenge with a young person's death. In the senseless deaths of children they, and we, feel a deep sense of wrongness, and a wish to make things right.

We are not entirely altruistic in this, for the deaths of children detract from our own ability to be hopeful. In order for our lives to be meaningful we need to feel that there is a future, and children do not have to be our own to be 'the future generation'. We all need the promise, especially after a tragedy, that life will still provide us with renewal, with, if you like, a resurrection.

The loss of a partner tests our ability to submit ourselves again to life in a search for renewal through the affection and love of another person. In this sense it gives many of us the chance to grow eventually through loving someone else. The death of a child tests our love in a different way. It tests our love of life itself. It tests our faith, our belief in innocence and in ourselves as custodians of what is good. What it offers us is the opportunity to become wiser parents, and wiser adults for other children.

* * *

CHAPTER 3

Objects of Desire

'Ghosts' within possessions. How a journey from the inside out has some strange accomplices

When someone dies, the love or passion felt for them is often, for a short time, transferred on to the objects which belonged to them. For most people possessions assume a temporary importance after a death, an importance which they did not previously have. This is part of the grieving process. Objects become temporary ambassadors. Records, books, shirts, shoes, a pair of gloves, a bottle of perfume can become almost a representation of the dead person or, in the case of a parting, the person who has gone away.

They then become transitional objects between the past and the future and have the function of allowing us the time we need for commemoration of what has gone, and for adjustment towards what is to come. It would seem that in being dispossessed of a person, we must possess ourselves of their objects as a form of comfort or compensation. It is almost as if we love the person's belongings or objects for a while instead of the person.

This happens to children in a pronounced way because of the importance of toys and objects in their daily lives, and the way they use them as part of their imaginative play. A colleague told the following story of what happened with his eight-year-old daughter when her grandmother, his wife's mother, died recently. Although the child was not very close to her grandmother, she cried when she was told the news, and then went out to stand by the pond in the garden.

Her father asked her what she would like to do, what she would like to happen to say goodbye to her granny. She said she would like to float some things on the pond, so together they did this. They floated a candle on the pond because that seemed right, and then they thought up a game to remember the things which reminded them of Granny, which typified her. Using the child's toys as objects, they sent a miniature kettle on its way, a tiny TV set, a cup and saucer and a telephone. Then the child remembered that Gran's flat had contained many pictures of her granddaughter, the child herself. But she did not want these floated; she wanted them put up on the garden wall.

By the time some pictures of her were on the garden wall the child was happy again. Life's optimistic balance had been restored. The dead had floated away, properly remembered, the smiling face of the future, the next generation, was propped up for all to see and the journey from tears to laughter was speedily accomplished. An inventive but also a truthful use of objects had helped bring about healing. It is important that the child did not float anything on the pond that did not describe her grandmother.

The pace at which the objects can 'float away' and not be missed is slower in adults. It can take weeks, months and even years to face clearing out a wardrobe full of clothes. For one man it has taken five years, and is not yet completely resolved; his dead wife's clothes are in the attic. She had asked him before she died not to get rid of them, and while he has managed to move them first of all into the spare room, then into the loft, he is still faced with the quandary of what he does when he sells the house.

A woman in her seventies spoke of having to 'put out' her dead husband's clothes to be collected because she could not hand them over herself. Even then, she took them back once. 'I rang up Oxfam, and they said they would collect them, and after I'd put them out I had to take them back in. It was a few weeks later before I rang them again and said I was ready this time.' Like many people, she had let her husband's possessions go a bit at a time.

In a sudden death or parting between adults what is left of the person in terms of the objects which typified them, or which they touched, wore or enjoyed, has an extra importance. The objects provide a temporary bridge between who has gone and what remains. They become part of the grieving process. Even a smell attached to an object matters. A woman in her thirties whose lover died suddenly, more than a decade ago, in a road accident said: 'I went through the whole laundry-basket picking up his clothes and holding them to my face, smelling them, smelling *him*.' When the TV series *Edge of Darkness* was shown some years afterwards she found herself in floods of tears over a sequence where the bereaved father reaches into the cupboard where his dead daughter's clothes are hanging, and holds them to his face. 'Troy Kennedy Martin, who wrote that, must have lost somebody abruptly himself, otherwise he wouldn't know that. He wouldn't know that that's what you do.'

She now has the series on video and watches it from time to time because she enjoys it and because that sequence still means so much to her as an affirmation of her own actions. 'People aren't honest about grief or, let's put it this way, the people who suffer it are, but you have to keep quiet because of taboos and prejudices.'

The other thing she did for a few weeks after her lover's death was to keep the same sheets on the bed. 'I can remember trying to retain his smell in the bed. It goes, of course, but for a while I wanted to hold on to that and I didn't wash the sheets until I was ready to.'

Finding comfort in the transient 'presence' of someone through their possessions – even their clothes in the laundry-basket – brings up fears about primitive or unacceptable behaviour. It is in primitive cultures, though also in established religions, that objects are imbued with extra meaning. For people in grief to give objects extra meaning for a few days, weeks or months threatens concepts of rational, civilised behaviour. This is one of the many prejudices against grief, and against the often passionate, wild nature of the grieving process some people undergo. As the woman above added: 'To admit in so-called polite company to smelling a dead lover's clothes threatens people. But they can't really have loved – at least not passionately – if they don't know that when someone who was in your bed one morning never again returns, you forget conventional behaviour. You want that person back, and if that can't happen you hang on to whatever there is left of them until you're ready to let go. That's a reality. At least it was *my* reality.'

This woman's reality was a passionate one because her relationship with her lover had been passionate. Not all griefs are passionate, because not all relationships are. Of the ones that are very intense, though, the prejudice against expressing them in passionate terms is powerful. Passion is something which frightens us, and which many of us go to great lengths to repress or avoid. But since we also sense that passion is a force to be reckoned with, we have found a way of defusing it. We do this through religion. Religion is a means by which we can funnel passion away from individual lives into the broader avenue of a congregation. People's individual voices are channelled into a congregational one, and passion is, supposedly, made safer. Religions of all denominations have been avenues for people's passions and longings for scores of centuries, and have taken over the way in which life and death are viewed and recognised.

Religions decree that in the final analysis responsibility for the deep meanings of life and death do not lie within individual hearts or consciences. They lie within the conventions laid down in books like the Bible, the Koran and the Talmud and in places like mosques, temples and churches. Religion relieves an individual of certain responsibilities, and imposes others. Religions say that one's life and one's heart belong to a god, and that this duty transcends earthly love.

The fact that within religion itself one can be Catholic, Methodist, Buddhist, Hindu, Muslim, Baptist, Taoist or Unitarian shows that no one religious way is right or true for everyone. What all these religions, barring Taoism, have in common, however, and what they offer within love or passion for their god, is their own investment in objects. All major conventional religions make some objects sacred. In other words, they invest in objects either a symbolic or an actual representation of a physically absent person or deity. Be it a cross, a communion wafer, a star, a crescent, a lamp or a universal candle, objects are imbued with meaning.

This shows that investing objects with meaning is something we have chosen to sanction and to systemise, as we have chosen to systemise passion. It thus has a precedent, and is not, in itself, bizarre. It is not something, in itself, that need be feared, and would only be a cause for concern if it were taken to extremes.

Giving objects meaning is something which all healthy children do. Children, from when they are tiny, form attachments to sometimes quite strange objects like the corner of a none-too-clean blanket or the left ear of a bear that has seen better days. It would therefore not seem inappropriate for adults to do this in their own way too.

Since so much of serious loss involves death, and since so many people need the transitional comfort of an object belonging to the dead person, it is important to see this need as valid, and to see the passion within it as valid. People who are not conventionally religious fear behaving in unusual ways, forgetting perhaps that this is something which worshippers in churches, mosques and temples do all the time. They speak out loud in a public place to an invisible person.

Fear of the power of objects can sometimes lead people to dispose of them too quickly. The objects are obviously painful reminders, and the feelings they provoke make some people wish to clear them away prematurely. The rational explanation for this is that people are 'tidying up' and 'keeping busy' and 'taking their mind off things'. But while fierce emotions need utilising as well as understanding, utility can be practised at the expense of empathy.

This happened with a woman in her seventies whose husband died after forty-five years of marriage. She bustled around straight after the death, got busy 'doing' and tidying, and then suddenly found she had 'tidied her husband away': 'Even before the funeral, I'd thrown all his little things away. I'd cut him off, and he'd gone, just like that.'

She feels that the day he was suddenly taken ill she 'did the wrong thing' through being too practical. Instead of holding his hand and talking to him, she tidied the room so the ambulance people would not find it in a mess (even though it was already tidy). 'I've cried and cried about that. It was the last time I saw him conscious, and I was worrying about whether there were a few things lying around – and whether he had clean pyjamas to take to hospital.'

The wish to be practical can be a cover-up rather than a help and can conflict with the deeper needs of grief, as a man who was thirteen when his mother was killed found. Immediately following her sudden death her possessions were swiftly dispersed. He found this very upsetting, for he had formed strong emotional attachments to these possessions because they were all that remained of her. He needed time, therefore, to learn to part from them, and because of practical considerations was not given it.

He is now twenty and still recalls clearly the week after the Saturday morning when his mother was killed by a lorry while riding her bicycle. He was the only child of a single parent. Thankfully, he was close to his mother's brother and sister-in-law, who took over when his mother died. But within days of the death they began to move belongings out of the small house where mother and son had lived. The house was full of books, records and antiques which the dead woman had collected. Her son watched as, bit by bit, these objects were taken away from the place where he was born, and had spent all of his life: 'People started coming in and taking things, and I thought, slowly and surely our life – my mother's and mine – is being taken away. My mother's life was being fragmented down. It was all going away from me in books, records, plants, all the ornaments, they were all going, never to be returned. People who didn't bother with us when she was alive were taking things, all for the good reason that my aunt and uncle didn't want things wasted. So they asked people who knew her to take what they wanted. People who didn't bother with us when she was alive were taking things, and a lot of her life was being taken away from me.'

Seven years after his mother's death this man still feels that what happened was 'a bad mistake', that it has affected his ability to remember or reconstitute his mother in his mind. While he continues to live with his aunt and uncle, and is grateful to them for all they have done for him, he regrets what happened. In the years following her death he grieved not only for his missing mother, but for her missing memory, which he has tried hard to hold on to. It is this that concerns him, his wish to recapture his mother clearly, so that she does not vanish as if she had never existed. He believes that the abrupt removal of so many of her possessions contributed to this: 'Things we had bought together were going. It felt like the things were being killed, and as each bit left the house she was fading. She wasn't as strong in the house a week after she died. Her presence was going slowly away . . . '

His aunt and uncle, thinking they were acting for the best, decided he was 'young enough to put it all behind him', and did not, after an initial period of a few months, spend much time talking about his mother. In the last five years they have not talked of her at all. For a few years, until he was about sixteen, he kept his mother's memory alive in bed at night, speaking to her in his head, crying, saying things like 'This isn't working [living with his aunt and uncle], I wish you were still here.' He admits: 'I tried every day to talk to her, but she was slipping out of my mind . . . '

He now finds his mother's presence in his life faint, and he wishes for stronger, more frequent thoughts and images of her. He reproaches himself because he does not think of her often enough. About a year after his mother died he had a dream in which his aunt and uncle appeared as 'bad' people. He felt guilty about the dream, because his guardians are, in fact, good people, who he thinks have done well in bringing him up and in taking care of him. But in the dream his aunt and uncle knew his mother was still alive – shut away in a mental hospital. His mother was in pain because she knew her son was alive, but not with her. His aunt and uncle did not want to have anything to do with her any more, and would not tell her son where she was.

The sense of being 'undone' by a grief or a loss is profound, and can occur in many ways, some of them not at all obvious. With the man just mentioned it was the 'undoing', or unravelling, of the place where he and his mother lived which caused him pain by diminishing, he believes, his ability to remember his mother. It was the too swift removal of her possessions and the dismantling of the home they shared together which prevented the important remembrance.

In the process of moving from being undone to 'putting themselves back together again', objects – or signs – are a rite of passage for some people. They were for a mother in her sixties when faced with the death of a 35-year-old daughter. She began by explaining the depth of her grief, of having a strong urge to lie face down over her daughter's coffin, refusing to leave it. She then revealed how, through objects belonging to her daughter's children, she managed to travel back towards her own life again. 'At my age you don't expect to get over it, but you still have to carry on living, especially for the grandchildren. It's been two years since she died and I remember how I didn't want to leave her coffin. I would like to have been buried with her. It was the grandchildren who brought me back, them and their toys. I know this will sound daft, but for a long time after she died I cared more about those toys than the children did. I used to sit in the chair and talk to them sometimes when the children weren't here. They were a comfort to me.'

She talked to the bears, the dolls and the soft toys as she went about her daily chores. She took them out of the box of play things she kept for her grandchildren and sat them in a row on the sideboard. Every now and then she would pick one up and say something like 'You miss her too, don't you?'

A friend from down the road came in one day – she lives in the kind of village where people walk into each other's houses – and caught her at it. The friend asked her who she was talking to, and at that point the game was up: 'I laughed and said: "That lot", nodding towards the sideboard. She looked at me sideways, as if I was getting a bit odd, and there and then I took them down and put them back in the toy box.'

This mother thinks that the toys served a purpose in allowing her to express something she felt was inexpressible – the grief of losing a daughter. Since her daughter had lived nearby and they had seen each other every day, the wound caused by her death was almost palpable. Her mother could tell the toys, day after day, for a number of months, what it was like.

She told the toys quite ordinary, domestic things, like the fact that it was this time of day her daughter would be coming in for a cup of tea. She also tearfully told them the deep things. She would stand and look at them, like a miniature jury on the sideboard, and say that she wished she herself had died instead. This is something she did not want to burden her husband and two other children with because they had griefs of their own to go through.

Her conversation with the toys took this mother from her daughter's coffin back to being a grandmother for her grandchildren, a mother to her two other children and a wife. In a strange way they acted, for her, almost as midwives between the cocooned, womblike state of wishing not to be alive and emerging into the world again. The parallel with birth here is not accidental, for many people felt their emerging from grief to be a rebirth. They thought of the loss of a loved one as closing part of themselves down, a part which had to find life again in a new way if their own lives were to continue. Very importantly, it seemed they had to make an adjustment between the 'old' life, which contained the person they loved, and the new life, which did not.

In that adjustment, or journey, some people found that objects were imbued with 'messages' as well as having the transitional function of go-betweens. For one couple, whose son was killed in an accident when he was in his early twenties, the 'strange behaviour' of certain objects was – and still is – a comfort to them.

The couple have a successful business partnership, and do not think of themselves as mystical. They both, however, found that sudden loss, and the grief which followed it, partly changed this. For a start, the husband consulted a medium even though before his son's death he would have called himself a complete sceptic: 'I was the biggest sceptic in the world. Honestly. I thought it was a load of hoo-ha.' His wife explained that she would have been more likely to think he was having an affair than visiting a medium. But the husband drew great comfort from his visit to 'one of this country's leading spiritualists': 'She was just so accurate about everything . . . the details of how he died, the fact that someone else was with him . . . How a woman could tell me the things she did I don't know . . . She told me not to worry about the argument we had before he left . . . She said he was fine . . . It's all very strange, I know, but she gave me a lot of comfort, and after having seen her I felt more at ease and relaxed than I'd done since he died. She helped me tremendously.'

The wife, who did not visit the medium, talked of drawing comfort in a different way, from the behaviour of certain objects. The first was the memorial candle which they lit in the house once a year. The first year it was lit, in the dining room, it smashed. 'I've spoken to loads and loads of people and nobody has had one smash . . . but M. [their son] was a very physical person. And the second year I thought it might smash again and I put it on a tray on the table and it burned a hole right through the tray and made a hole in the rubber mat underneath.'

She went on to describe the behaviour of other objects the night she insisted her husband take her to the graveyard before the stone was laid: 'He didn't want to take me because he knew I would get terribly upset, so he procrastinated and procrastinated. As a way of doing this, he took me to his mother's house on the way, and as we were standing there a cup just jumped out of the cupboard and fell at my feet.'

When challenged about the word 'jumped', she said: 'No, it *fell* out of the cupboard, but there was no reason for it to. She didn't have a lot of stuff, and it wasn't crammed in or anything. We were both very upset at the time . . . '

As they neared the graveyard that evening, instead of becoming more distressed, she became less so. They both did. When they stood by the grave, she turned to her husband and said, calmly: 'I feel nothing.' Her husband replied: 'No. He isn't here.' He meant this comment in a highly comforting way, not as a statement that their son was dead, but that the grave did not contain where he truly rested: 'If I took your jacket from you and put your jacket in a cupboard, that cupboard would represent the grave. But you're not in that jacket, are you? The essence of you is not in your jacket.' His wife took up the theme: 'It's not the grave that's important. That's what I was feeling. Whatever the spirit is, then that spirit is there for ever, and that laughter of that spirit, that aura, is still with you.'

After leaving the grave that evening they both visited the house of their other son's mother-in-law, where he and his wife were temporarily staying because builders were in their own home. While there, a toy that was standing on a shelf fell off and broke at their feet. When they went home that night, a bulb in a wall light at their bedside sprang out of its socket and, again, broke at their feet.

Their deduction from these three breakages during the evening they visited the grave together for the first time was that their son, who was a very physically robust and affectionate person, was trying to 'tell' them something. What? 'It's not the grave that's important,' the wife repeated. Her husband added: 'Someone is only truly dead when you forget them, and we remember him as he was, as *who* he was, and that's perhaps the deeper meaning of those incidents.'

In the 'reality' of the grieving process there is a broad spectrum of experience, much of which is not discussed in any company, let alone the so-called polite kind. The naked, truly sincere bits are left out. Ironically, this leaves the rest of us exposed: if people who have already suffered loss and grief will not tell the truth about it for fear of being called irreligious, superstitious or mad, how do the rest of us know what that truth is? How do the rest of us know what to do and where to follow? How do we know how to react if we want to take a dead person's shirt to bed with us? Is doing so a sign that we are crazed?

The answer seems to be that in the short term we need the objects, and could in fact be damaged by not 'loving' them if we wish to. Equally damaging would be to 'love' them too long, for they are not the person we have lost.

It is clear that the sudden arrival of grief, through an unexpected death or separation, can strip people of conventional behaviour, and leave them naked in the face of powerful emotions. It can make them weep in public, or cling in private to an object the lost person used or loved. It can make them smell clothes in the laundry-basket or visit mediums. The rest of us feel destabilised by such actions. We often express disapproval of them because they impinge on the safe, mundane boundaries that daily living requires and demands.

This then becomes circular. People in grief feel inhibited about expressing what they truly feel, or need. They do so because the rest of us might not recognise or understand them. The rest of us do not recognise or understand because we do not know. With the wish to relate to objects, as with so much else that surrounds grief and loss, there are complex reasons for keeping this secret. I have mentioned the fear of being called mad or irreligious. There is also the fear of being childish, something we view differently from the more pleasing quality of being childlike.

So much of our prejudice against grief is based on our prejudice against and fear of childhood. Outside religions, it is young children who invest objects with disproportionate or mystical properties. There is a fear, therefore, that an adult who does this is reverting to childish behaviour. We do not think the person might be drawing on highly creative childhood sources, but view it as possible infantile regression. We are worried that a person who was capable and responsible the day before her or his partner died, or left, is suddenly going to become an irresponsible, needy child. A therapist who works part-time for a bereavement counselling service explained that it makes us feel unsafe and anxious: 'This strikes fear into the rest of us because we think it might happen to us too. We think that whatever capable mantles we ourselves have built up can fall apart or be destroyed. This, I think, strikes at the root of why the rest of us don't know how to behave appropriately with people who have suffered severe loss. We want to say: "Oh, time will heal" or "You'll feel better tomorrow." We don't want to have to face someone else's temporary disintegration because it threatens our own often fragile sense of maturity and stability.'

In the journey from the interior of grief back to the exterior world which is impervious to individual loss, the combination of a temporary attachment to objects and childlike behaviour, such as crying or being unable to cope with adult tasks, is quite 'normal', according to this therapist: 'What would be abnormal would be for someone not to be affected. If you have loved somebody, and you lose them, you *should* be temporarily "undone".'

The wish to materialise or memorise a dead person, for example through holding on to objects that are still 'warm' from their touch or affection, means that some people become extraordinarily receptive during a time of grief. Jan, whose sister died suddenly twelve years ago, believes that their closeness made her 'aware' of the death. Jan recalls waking up early the morning her sister died, as if from a nightmare: 'I woke up at about 6 a.m. with a feeling of tremendous anxiety. I thought there must be burglars in the house, that I might have heard something which had woken me. After listening for a while I heard nothing more, but I still got up and searched the whole house to make sure everything was normal. I went back to sleep again, and it seemed I had just fallen into a deep sleep when this time I woke, and was on my feet before I had time to think. There had been a terrible crash, like a window being smashed, and I raced into the living room expecting to see glass all over the floor. My heart was pounding. At this stage I was still partly not fully awake. It felt as if I was half in and out of a nightmare. I just knew something dreadful had happened, but I had no idea what.'

The phone rang shortly after this, at seven, and it was her brother-in-law, giving her the awful news that her sister had died fifteen minutes previously. He said that having woken at six feeling inexplicably ill, she had got out of bed. She had paced up and down for a while and had then collapsed and died just as he was phoning for an ambulance.

Jan, who was in her mid-thirties when this happened, went straight round to her brother-in-law's house to find him sitting in the living room surrounded by broken glass. Her sister had collapsed on the glass coffee table and broken it. Jan had subsequently drawn great comfort from this. She joined together in her mind the broken glass table and her own nightmare of broken glass and felt a part of her sister's death rather than excluded from it: 'We were very close, and I gathered afterwards that she had collapsed at 6.45. That was the time I woke up the second time. I looked at the clock before going into the living room.

'What do I deduce from it? I believe my waking at the same time she did, and the sensation of smashing glass in my own house, made me a part of her death. I don't know how or why, and I don't need to know. What matters is that it has always been a tremendous comfort to me, then and now, to feel that I was involved, that she didn't die alone, without me knowing.'

Jan feels that this has also affected her memory of her sister or, more precisely, her ability to remember her with what she calls 'a kind of joyful sadness'. 'Having seen other friends lose people since then, I think one of the most difficult things is to carve out a place in yourself where the person can rest peacefully as part of your own memory. As part of that process you have to negotiate that whole business of "the death" itself. That can take quite a time, especially if the death has been violent, or if it happened after an argument.

'The reason why I was so helped by my own experience of a crash is that it joined me in some way in my sister's death and her "presence", the memory of her inside me is warm and safe.'

The wish to find 'good' in grief, to invest events with positive meanings and to find hidden significance in things like accidents rather than dismiss them simply as coincidences, can be interpreted in a number of ways.

First, there is obviously a religious interpretation. For those who believe firmly in an afterlife, the dead person is not truly dead at all and their 'presence' through signs is not only accepted, but almost sought.

Secondly, there is a psychoanalytic or psychological interpretation. A person's mind has received a terrible shock, and as part of the process of defending against that – and also of adjusting to it – the mind will choose to keep the dead person 'alive' just a little bit longer until it is ready to absorb the full weight of what has happened. Someone has gone, and a healthy, balanced survivor will seek to adjust or compensate for this. A method of compensation is to delay the shock of the departure by extending the life or significance of the dead person through objects.

Thirdly, there is also a possible 'noble' interpretation, which is that the search for meaning that most people are prone to in some way is evidence of a wish to make sense of death, as there is a wish to make sense of life. They are, essentially, the same quest, and to seek to imbue events with extra significance is, in a sense, a work of love and devotion. It is a wish to continue a relationship with the dead, to reflect upon them, to draw good from them, and through that to bring comfort to one's own life by the remembrance or celebration of another's. Artists do this through music, paintings and books.

A hospital chaplain, who is involved with death and bereavement every day of his working life, clarified the difference between the first and third interpretations, between religion and the search for meaning: 'People who are religious *practise* religion in some way, through the reading of holy texts or regular worship. People who search for meaning in life – and I think *all* people do that – are spiritual people. They may not practise any religion, but I think everyone has spiritual needs.

'At a time of bereavement my job is to help people look for meaning in life, and to look at what they believe. With people who are dying, and who are not religious, my job is to help them to review their life, because they need to set some kind of value on it. They need to know that their life has made a difference . . . The spiritual search for meaning is always there, even if it's not articulated.'

This search for meaning, and for the layers of meaning which open up once that search begins, gives an added texture to the lives of people left behind when someone close to them dies. As the state of being 'in love' can make the world look different through heightening our awareness, so the state of being in grief can make things look different too. With grief, though, it is more the ability to see 'into' or 'behind' things.

A woman in her forties described this 'deeper seeing' through grief which happened to her after the deaths, close together, of her mother, father and sister: 'The night my sister died I looked up at the sky, and I had never seen a sky like it before. It was deep red, and there were clouds scudding across it at great speed. They were flying across the heavens, and I drew enormous comfort from that. Exactly a year later to the night she died, looking up at the sky 200 miles away, it was the same. This wonderful red, and the clouds racing across . . . '

The wish to find meaning in the loss of loved ones can be expressed, therefore, in countless different ways: through objects, through music or through investing the sky with personal significance.

* * *

CHAPTER 4

Breaking the Faith

The difference between mourning a death and a divorce

The importance of objects of desire is that they carry the weight of our scorn or anger as well as our affection. They are things to break or simply dispose of, as well as things to love. Because of this, the difference between our treatment of the objects of a dead person and the objects of a living person who has, say, left us for someone else is usually considerable. Whereas we tend to value the former, we might well hurl the latter out of the window. The most mundane object belonging to a person who we cared for and who has died is often cherished. The most expensive object left by a person who has caused us grief through leaving us of their own volition is likely to be derided or destroyed.

There are countless film scenes of women or men flinging objects after their deserting partners. At their most extreme they can be highly amusing, as heated lavatory seats, tropical fish, pyjamas with motor cars on them and expensive porcelain go sailing out of top-floor windows, are offered at car boot sales or thrown at the wall.

We often ridicule the objects of a departing person who has had the bad taste to find us wanting and the bad grace to act on it. In our state of grief, we are made to feel worthless and so seek to make the objects which belonged to the person who has gone worthless in turn.

A man in his late thirties experienced this when his relationship with the woman he had lived with for fourteen years ended: 'I didn't want her to go, and if the truth was told, I couldn't let her go. I was still too in love with her, and she knew that, and took advantage of it. I spent a lot of money trying to get her back, sending her flowers, buying her presents . . . '

She had told him at first that she was leaving because she needed some time to be by herself. It was when he discovered there was another man involved that he began the process of getting angry. 'After she left I sat in the bedroom looking at her clothes. She'd taken loads with her, but she had so many, there was loads of stuff around. And I'd pick up a hairbrush on the dressing table or a perfume bottle, and just turn it round in my hand.

'I'd cried anyway when she'd gone, but when I discovered there was someone else, I sat in that room and just wept. It was awful to think of her with someone else. Then one day I just thought, I want all this lot out of here. I don't want anything of hers at all. I want her out.'

He 'sat on' this for a few days, his feelings fluctuating between deep sadness and anger. At one point he went into the bedroom and banged the hairbrush on the dressing table. 'I was really angry for a while, and I think I'd have liked to rip everything up.' What he did instead was much more satisfying from his point of view: 'I took a deep breath and decided another woman could have them. I'd get rid of her that way by giving her stuff away.' He packed it all up and took it to a charity shop. 'The woman in the shop thanked me and said how grateful they were for donations. And I found myself saying to her: "Don't thank me. I should thank you."'

This happened three years ago. In common with many people who have suffered pain from a break-up, this man sought professional help and saw a psychotherapist for eighteen months after the split. He is now in another committed relationship and says: 'For me it was important to give her clothes away so another woman could have them rather than rip them up. That would have meant she still had power over me. By giving them to someone else to use I think I was saying I would find someone else myself. That's why I felt good about it.'

Another issue that is different when we lose someone through abandonment rather than death is what we do about their secrets. We are not necessarily prepared to keep the secrets we shared while part of a couple if the person leaves us and breaks our trust. This can be a big difference in the ways we get over the grief involved in parting with a living person compared with a dead one: whether or not we keep the faith.

Marion, who is in her late fifties, enjoyed 'an amazing liberation' through not keeping the faith of her 35-year-long marriage which ended in divorce four years ago. 'Perhaps I was brought up to be particularly secretive or discreet, but I never discussed anything at all about our marriage. When I read revealing accounts in magazines or saw people on television talking about intimate things, I would just switch off.' This started to change when it became obvious to Marion that her husband was having an affair: 'What I found really hard to take was that he must have thought I was stupid not to notice. He smelled of perfume, he was away a lot on vague business meetings and he didn't even bother to cover his tracks.'

For about a year she did not say anything, but she noticed her attitude to intimate secrets altered. She began to read magazines avidly, and lapped up TV programmes about marriage, relationships and sexuality. 'It was odd, really. There he was nipping in and out of our bed thinking I was ignorant of what was happening, and I was beginning to learn a lot about life.'

What Marion learned was that her marriage had never been sexually satisfying any more than it had been satisfying in other ways. Even though they were not divorced at that stage, Marion joined a group for older 'singles' and found herself 'spilling the beans' about her unsatisfactory marriage: 'I don't think I'd ever said the word "sex" in public before, but there I was in a group of people saying that my husband was having an affair and had never been a good enough husband to me anyway.'

Another woman, who is now in her early forties, talked of the difference between death and 'divorce' within a relationship that was passionate. Unlike Marion's, however, her initial feeling on being told by her husband that he was leaving her was one of intense physical pain: 'It was a bit like a punch in the stomach, although I've never experienced that – but more like someone thrusting, plunging a spear into me. *Twenty years* is how long we'd been together. He meant everything to me. I worshipped him. I worshipped his body. He was the only man I'd slept with and we'd been together since I was fifteen and he was sixteen.'

While most people interviewed saw divorce or separation as being more jagged than death, and as producing feelings that were initially more difficult to disperse or process, this woman felt differently: 'There *is* a difference between divorce and death – an important one. If he'd died, I would have built an idol out of his memory. I would never have looked for someone else to replace him.'

For a number of years after her husband left her for someone much younger, this woman did not even think about another relationship. Now she is ready to. 'If he'd died, I wouldn't have learned what I have. I'd have sat at home, and built a kind of shrine to his memory. No one would have been able to match him in my eyes. I can laugh about that now. Looking back on it, I've learned a lot. Before Tony left, my sense of identity depended on him. When he went, it was shattered. Now it belongs to me.

'How did I get here? I think I crawled the first bit. I couldn't even care if I washed. I didn't give a damn what I looked like. And for a year I saw a counsellor, a bereavement counsellor. I thought they were only for when someone died, but a friend got an appointment for me. I found that really helped. I saw a woman. I couldn't have faced a man.

'In one way death [her husband's] would have been "cleaner". I wouldn't have suffered in the way I did, but then neither would I think like I do now. I've joined a singles group, and I'm not trying to find someone to match Tony – I'm looking for someone better!'

When establishing another relationship after a divorce, a marriage guidance counsellor emphasised how important it is to take time off between one relationship and another. In her experience second marriages often 'came to grief' faster than first ones if people did not stop and assess what had happened to the first relationship before moving into the second. 'If people do not stop to recognise and to evaluate their own part in the relationship that has broken up, they remain unchanged by what has happened. They take the same person into the second marriage as they left the first one with. They expect a new relationship to fix their hurt, rather than doing some fixing of their own first.

'If you cannot recognise your own hurt or wounds, then you will carry on with them, and take them wholesale somewhere else. The shock of finding problems appearing so quickly in a second marriage breaks that relationship too.'

These prevailing wounds, or jagged edges, are what can make recovery from relationship break-ups more protracted than getting over a death. A man in his early fifties who recently retired from a senior management position spoke about this. A few years before retiring he discovered his wife had been having an affair with another man. He forgave her, but within months of retiring was 'devastated' to learn that the relationship was still continuing behind his back: 'I went through absolute hell. I loved her dearly, and I didn't want it to happen, I didn't want to let go of the marriage. So I took her back when I first found out, and we had a fresh start. Or so I thought . . . '

When he realised the relationship with another man had not ended, he went through a year of many different griefs, one of which he describes as the loss of the person he believed his wife to be: 'It wasn't just the adultery, it was the fact that I had been deceived by what she was, by *who* she was. She was someone I discovered I didn't truly know, and her promises, her words, were only as good as the circumstances they were fitted into. I found out she had been like this since before we had met, someone who was not capable of keeping her word. I knew she was a bit insecure, and I thought I could make that better for her by providing her with security and with everything she needed. It didn't work.'

The loss of his wife to another man has since deepened in his mind to include other losses within their relationship. He felt, for example, that he had suffered grief through the loss of the knowledge of another person, of the certainty of who the person is. Since his wife no longer seemed the person he thought she was, her actions were all the more shocking to him. 'It is grief for a devastating loss of trust. I simply had believed that this could not happen. I trusted my wife and loved her. I did not believe she was capable of that level of deceit. At the time we parted I had not stopped loving her, and I haven't yet recovered from the ending of the marriage. I still feel an enormous sense of loss, and there is as well the fact that I know she is still alive – with someone else.' For this man, trust is 'the most important thing in your life'. He considers it the most valuable part of a relationship, because a relationship could not be built on or sustained without it.

Much the same thing was said by a woman whose husband committed suicide when they were both in their late twenties. Eight years later she is only just beginning to feel good again. 'If someone takes their life away from you like that, you're left with terrible feelings. You don't think there's anything, or anybody, in the world you can trust. What you end up doing is not trusting *yourself*.'

She had felt tremendous guilt for five or six years following her husband's death, and had not realised until about eighteen months ago how this had affected not only her view of life itself, but even her ability to breathe: 'I couldn't trust anything again. I just couldn't bear the thought of anything or anyone hurting or rejecting me ever again. I wasn't even breathing properly, I was only letting a little bit of air into my body.'

Her recovery did not begin until she discovered how angry she was about this: 'I didn't start to get better until I started to get angry, really angry, with what he'd done to me, and all the years I'd spent being guilty and afraid.' During those years she thought her husband's death was her own fault, and she constantly blamed herself for it. She also felt a terrible failure that seven years after her husband's suicide she was still 'not well'. She had read books on grief which told her there were stages to go through, and that they took certain times. She was taking longer, and it made her afraid.

This changed when she went into adult education to study for a part-time degree course. She began to go out into the world of learning and to meet other people who were learning too. 'It gave me confidence in myself, and it's been good from then. I've got my confidence and my trust back, and I'm smiling again. Sometimes I just like breathing, I like going out into the garden, looking at the night sky and just feeling how good it is to trust life again, to let air come in and out of my body. And I feel that I'm lucky enough to be healthy, and that life is sweet. I just really appreciate life, and simple things like breathing.'

The opposite of this openness is described by a man who feels constricted by the recent break-up of a relationship, so much so that he does not trust himself to be alone. He is twenty-four, and so devastated by the loss of a four-year relationship, ended by the woman he was living with, that he does not lead what he calls 'a normal life'. Rather than return to an empty flat he goes to the pub instead: 'I just can't be on my own. I don't know what I'm frightened of, what I think will happen, but I don't go home till it's closing time. Each morning I get up with a thick head . . . At weekends I go to the pub lunchtime as well.'

The loss of trust, in other people and in oneself, in one's ability to be alone, to breathe, to live normally, is fundamental to the grief surrounding the acrimonious or one-sided ending of a relationship. By rejecting us and making us feel, if not exactly worthless, then certainly 'not good enough', a person who voluntarily leaves can cause us untold grief which can mean a departure is more destructive than a death. For although death involves the absolute removal of a loved one, it does not usually break a trust. And where trust in a person we have invested in is broken, it can shake our trust in ourselves, and in the world we live in. In explaining this a counsellor says: 'Trust is crucial, critical, to everything about our lives. When it is broken, it undermines our faith in the living, and in life itself.' We invest trust in objects around us, as well as in people: 'Trust in objects underpins practically every human action. One trusts – expects – cups to hold coffee, aeroplanes to fly, the ground to stay still beneath one's feet, and people to do as they say they will and to be who they say they are. Where these things do not happen, it causes anger or small pain on a minor scale, like when the coffee cup deposits scalding coffee on your lap, and catastrophe of awful proportions when planes crash or earthquakes swallow up the lives of thousands of people.

'Outside war, trust in the shape and stability of daily objects like chairs or walls is essential to living a normal, sane life. On a personal level, where trust is abused, sanity itself – and the ability to love – is threatened. Whether it be the deep scars formed by child abuse, which is one of the most basic betrayals of trust, or the pain of adult deception, having trust broken threatens all future relationships. Basically, it threatens our faith in human nature and therefore in ourselves.'

When trust is not kept and faith, therefore, is broken, anger is part of the healing process. While often painful to experience, it provides the energy and the impetus to make us do something, change something or move on. Anger is accentuated when a relationship is lost not by death, but by design. In the case of a death the 'anger' component does not usually last long, for it is overtaken by remorse and genuine sadness. When we suffer a heavy loss because the person we were once committed to leaves us for someone else, or just leaves, anger is our rescuer. Where it is not called upon to do its job, we are left in more trouble, as was the case for one woman in her mid-thirties. It took her many years to get over the ending of a relationship she had had with a man who went back to the USA a year after they had become lovers. For the next six months they corresponded, and she then went to stay with him for a month. Before setting off she had made the difficult decision that she was prepared to move to the USA permanently to be with him – and suffer the professional consequences of leaving behind a good job she would not be able to replace.

When she arrived in California, it was to find that the relationship was over. He said that as her arrival drew near he had not wanted to tell her on the phone, or in a letter. There was already someone else. He met her at the airport as if nothing had happened: 'I thought it was odd he didn't kiss me, but I thought he was saving it till we were alone.' He still did not have the courage to tell her, and it was not until hours later that she confronted him – and learned the truth: 'I went into a corner of the room and I collapsed in a heap. I wanted to scream and I put my fist in my mouth to stop myself. He just sat there. He didn't touch me. I wanted to rent my clothes, to rip them and scream and scream, and I couldn't, because our culture doesn't allow us to do that. We're not allowed to let it out. So I got drunk instead. It happens all the time, it's a standard practice, a shorthand in plays and films, that's how you express strong emotions, you reach for the bottle.'

Although she held a highly responsible job at the time – and still does – within months of returning from the West Coast she found herself unable to work due to terrible head and face pains. 'I began to think I was going mad. I went through every test you can think of, and this pain wouldn't go away. I ended up so disorientated that one day I found myself in the bizarre situation where I thought I was going to see a dentist, and it turned out I was seeing a psychiatrist. I looked at this woman and said to her: "That's a peculiar question for a dentist to ask." She told me she wasn't a dentist, and that in her opinion the pain I was getting was due to severe stress, and she recommended me to see a psychotherapist.'

This woman was in therapy for three years before she felt fully well again: 'I learned I came from a family where we keep things in, like rats in a cage. I had a whole history of bottling up bad times, and by the time this happened to me [the shock in California] it was cumulative.

'If you don't get rid of pain or grief at the time – the natural time when it should be got rid of – if you're not given the right learning and the right conditioning, then it stays with you. With me it had built up and built up over years. It took two years of therapy before I even got angry with this man over the fact that I went all the way to California to be kicked in the teeth. Where was my anger at the time? Why hadn't I let rip at *him*?

'It all went inwards instead of outwards. I had a very physical response to what happened. I remember hurting everywhere, a real physical hurt which I wanted to get away from, and at times I felt as if I was strangling, as if there was nothing to make my voice come out, nothing inside me to push it.'

Although she did not go into therapy because of this relationship, but because of her unexplained physical symptoms, she has discovered the link between the two: 'To give it its simplest phrase, I bottle things up, and everything that was happening to me was getting stored. The facial pain was a symptom, it was the result of whatever was wrong in my life and was always going to be wrong in my life unless I actually got some help.'

This woman had also lost two grandparents she loved deeply when they had both died in their eighties. Of the difference between a death and the ending of a relationship, she says: 'If somebody you love dies, really it's got nothing to do with you. It's an accident, it's out there, and it's not your fault. But if it's a relationship that ends, then something happens inside you, and you think, was it something to do with you, weren't you good enough? And it's easy then to turn the anger that happens with the grief inwards.

'You think it's because of something you've done, or something you haven't done, it's some standard you haven't met, this ideal person you could be if only you tried harder. Also it's the idea that the person can come back. Perhaps if you change . . . You have the feeling that perhaps if you do something else, you will have that love back again.

'I think sudden death holds lots of regrets, like if you had an argument, or didn't have time to say goodbye or tell someone you loved them. But when the person is still alive, the question of what you can do about it hangs on. I couldn't believe that he didn't love me, and I wanted him back because I still loved him . . . and my thought was maybe if I was patient, and didn't get angry, and was understanding, this might happen. That's where my anger went.'

In the journey from inner despair back out into the world again most people find there are obstacles to be overcome. There are 'rapids' to negotiate, lonely bridges to cross or mountains of anger to scale. With a death, these emotions can usually find their way, and begin their healing, unimpeded by any real hopes that the dead person might return. In the case of a separation it is more difficult for these emotions to get clearly, and cleanly, to work.

A man in his mid-forties went through a year of ambivalence before he finally walked out on a relationship that had been destructive for a number of years. He and the woman he had lived with for a decade had tried many 'small partings', breaks from each other and separate holidays. It was not until he cleared all his possessions out of the house which she owned, however, that a clean break took place: 'It was dark, about eight o'clock at night, and I'd put everything I owned in the car – books, shelving, the lot. And I suddenly looked at the car piled high with stuff, and I thought, I'm forty-six years old and all my life is in the car.' He said it was the jolt of realising this, of seeing his life, symbolised by his possessions, all bundled up ready to be driven away on four wheels, that enabled him finally to make the break emotionally: 'Up until then I kept on hoping, kept on thinking that things would change. But I had to drive away for that to happen.'

Sometimes separation from another person is more difficult than death because in most cases a death is not decided upon, whereas separation is; it can lead to misgivings that persist – even worse. Frank, now in his mid-fifties, feels that the death of his father would have been easier to bear than a thirty-year separation which eventually culminated in their meeting again. Frank is Polish and came to this country as a fourteen-year-old refugee, a survivor of Auschwitz. His grandmother, mother and sister were killed in the camp, but his father, who fought in the army, survived. He would have had no idea that Frank was still alive, for he would have believed him killed along with the rest of the family.

Frank, meanwhile, became a rich businessman. As a Jewish child arriving in Britain without a family but with a strong gift for survival, he became streetwise. He started with a market stall and worked his way up from there. Throughout all this time he carried a picture of his young father in army uniform in his wallet. He was never without it. Dutifully he looked at this picture a number of times a day.

Frank believes his eventual search for his father was based on his bond with this object, the photograph he carried in his wallet. The hunt started when Frank's own two children were born when he was in his late twenties. His need for family ties, to introduce his small children to the man in the picture – if he was still alive – became a quest. Frank began contacting international organisations for help in trying to trace his father.

It took almost twenty years, but the Red Cross eventually found him. He was living in a tenement building in New York City, and had remarried. Frank was divorced by this time and living on his own, both his children having left home. He flew out to see his father – and the problems then began: 'I was looking for him at the airport, but he wasn't there to meet me, so I went to the address. It was terrible. The place was dirty. He was dirty and stooped over, with no pride in himself, and he hardly spoke English. He had been in America all this time, and he hadn't learned the language.

'It was difficult for us to communicate. He drank a lot, and the TV was on loud all the time so I had to shout practically. He didn't seem interested in the pictures I showed him of his grandchildren. We were like strangers. There was such a big difference between us. I had wanted him to be proud of me, of what I had achieved, and it seemed to mean nothing to him. I thought if we were on our own, if I brought him to London, things might be better.'

The father's trip to London a month later, paid for by Frank, was a disaster. Frank had left him with plenty of money, enough to buy half a dozen good suits, but his father arrived at Heathrow looking as shabby as he had done a month earlier. According to his son, his manners were non-existent and he was uninterested in anything except television. He did not want to meet his grown-up grandchildren or to hear anything about his son's successful business. He did not want to go out to restaurants, to listen to music or to hear about any aspect of his son's life. He had nothing to say about his own life, either about all the missing years or about his day-to-day activities.

When Frank drove his father back to the airport, they could barely meet each other's eyes. There was, for the middle-aged son, nothing to see in his father's gaze. There was no meeting point, just a terrible emptiness. In the end there was nothing honest or heartfelt to say, nor any real way, therefore, of saying goodbye. They walked away from each other, two figures at an airport who would never meet again.

The disappointment has broken Frank. The shattering of hope and trust contained in all those years of building a successful business with his father's picture in his wallet has defeated him. He has now sold his business, and leads a semi-reclusive life. He does not wish to become close to anyone again, or to have anyone become close to him, for he feels that what happened with his father was worse than divorce, worse than death: 'If he had died, I could remember him as he was, a young man in an army uniform. I wish he had stayed a picture in my wallet.'

Frank now has no idea whether his father is dead or alive. Frank has moved, and, after receiving no reply to a few short transatlantic notes he sent, has given up. The non-relationship between himself and his father, he says, is 'worse than the camps, worse than anything that's ever happened to me'. The circumstances surrounding this tragedy are obviously extreme. It is shocking for anyone to be abandoned or rejected by a close relative, and in Frank's case the rejection demolished years of hope. But Frank's emotional investment in the picture of his father was high, perhaps higher than he realised. When his wish to celebrate the bringing to life of this picture was brusquely rejected, he was unable to accept how different his father was from his image.

The absence of celebration which follows most partings is what distinguishes them from most deaths. While the death itself is not celebrated, the person is, and remains or grows in our memories. We are the custodians of these memories, and when a person leaves us through a death, they do not (barring suicide) break faith with us. Memories of them can then remain and develop in us as part of our inner landscapes. People who have died remain loved. People who have left do not. We might, in time, re-form friendly relationships with them because they are the mothers or fathers of our children, or because they are our mothers or fathers. But if they have rejected us, a part of us often remains more hurt by this than we realise. At the very least we are wary.

If relationships with the person who has rejected us continue in some form, they may have a 'dead-end' quality to them. They might continue because we need to negotiate over shared property, or over access to children. They might also continue because we are too frightened to leave them. In the cases of partners who have deceived or rejected us, we tend to stay because we cannot bring ourselves to break long ties, or to face loneliness. If we do stay, though, there are usually so many closed-off avenues, so many culs-de-sac, and so much spontaneity that cannot be allowed. A counsellor believes these 'dead' relationships between living people are much more damaging than actual death: 'At least death is not your fault – or not usually – and it physically removes someone from you. It gives you a *chance*. When people are stuck in relationships which bring out the worst in both of them and they can't find a way out, it's dreadful. They can't see clearly, and they can go on and on for years not seeing clearly, and then sometimes it's too late. They're too old, or too dependent . . . They feel they've wasted their lives.'

Being stuck in a 'dead' relationship is a kind of living death where one's 'better' self, the alert, affectionate and spontaneous qualities we all possess to some degree, is shut off, as if in a coffin. As we defend ourselves against an actual death, so we defend the more precious aspects of ourselves against a dead-end relationship. We shut away our treasures, either because we resent the person we are with, and do not think they deserve our better selves, or because the relationship is, quite simply, bad, and does not encourage the best in us.

In closing off the parts of ourselves which are valuable, we do not realise that this eventually hurts us more than the person we are with. Neither do we realise how much this partitioning of ourselves makes us, ironically, more dependent, not less, on the person we are angry with. This often leads us to become committed to dead-end relationships long after they have ended. The counsellor spoke of the number of people he has worked with who, although divorced, are not emotionally separated: 'I used to be astounded – and I mean *astounded* – at the grief caused by this. You'd get some people who came to see you who'd be describing something an ex-partner did which annoyed them and you'd say to yourself, but wait a minute, they've lived at opposite ends of the country for five years. What is this?' It became clear to him that emotional dependency or entanglement did not end with a closed door, a packed suitcase or a change of address: 'If you want to talk about unresolved grief, the kind that means you can't get on with the rest of life, then there's a great deal of it in people who have divorced. It's because people don't take time. They expect to be over it in a few weeks or a few months, and they bury a lot of stuff. That stuff stays hidden like toxic waste, if you like, and it eventually comes out in all kinds of needy or bitter behaviour . . . '

The reason why it can be more difficult to lose a relationship through something like divorce is that the lost person is not celebrated, but castigated. Not until the anger has gone is it possible for the person left behind to begin the creative process of building a life based on positive rather than negative feelings.

* * *

CHAPTER 5

'Have a Happy Day'

A broad view of the causes of grief, and how these can affect and inform individual losses

While the loss of an important relationship through death or separation causes us grief in a direct way, losses of other kinds play an important role in informing us about grief. As adults we read, watch and listen to the news which brings daily reports of tragedies near and far and, although these are other people's direct griefs and not our own, they often affect us. They move us to write letters, like the thousands of people in Northern Ireland and the Republic who wrote to the Parrys, the couple who lost their son in the IRA bombing in Warrington. They move us to act on other people's behalf: to lay flowers outside a football stadium, to take part in a vigil for a victim of torture or to raise money for a child's wheelchair through a sponsored walk. We do this from compassion, but compassion which is formed in us by an understanding of the grief of others.

The compassion that we feel for others is an important part of our wish to share the burden of pain which grief brings, and to develop through others a sense of our own boundaries. It provides evidence that we are not completely isolated in our despair, but are experiencing emotions other people have suffered too. It enables us to be part of a two-way process where we can give comfort and also receive it. We can give warmth and understanding to a stranger, and be warmed and moved in return by the understanding and good wishes of strangers.

Our general compassion is also an acknowledgement that the causes of grief are broader and deeper than an individual loss or death. We can feel grief for another person's loss, we can feel communal grief and we can also feel general sorrow for something like a war or famine, even if it is happening in another continent.

The causes of grief are therefore broad and, like our reactions to grief of all kinds, are suffered or understood more by some people than by others. War is a cause of grief, as is political expediency. Grief can be caused by legislation which allows or encourages exploitation, or by greedy, exploitative people abusing fair-minded legislation. In a world as complex as ours, the causes of grief are intricately linked.

An aid worker who spends much of her time in the Third World and is a field manager for one of this country's largest charities believes greed is the root cause of the suffering she sees: 'Whether it's telling breast-feeding mothers in Africa that they should spend their money buying powdered milk they can't afford, or whether it's making fortunes out of selling weapons, greed is the motive. Whether people are greedy for money or for power, it doesn't make much difference to starving people, but those seem to be the two things people will kill – or cause starvation – for.'

Another person involved in aid work, a man in his seventies who is a consultant to numerous Third-World aid programmes, says: 'So much grief in the Third World is avoidable. There *are* the resources, but there isn't the political sense. If you tolerate the idea of unrestrained capitalism, then taken to its logical conclusion grief is the result. For if profit is the motive, then of course you are going to take short cuts, and flatten land which then can't serve you, or ordinary people, in the future.

'There has to be an understanding of the future consequences of today's profits. A drug company can make a fortune in Africa or India today or tomorrow, and leave the people far worse off than they were before. If, as a culture, we condone those kinds of quick profits, then we need to learn what the result of them really is. Put succinctly, it's a lot of money for a few people, at the expense of dignity and self-sufficiency for many.'

The grief and heartache that result from placing a higher value on money than on qualities like honesty and compassion cannot be underestimated. The quick profits of bogus or unsuitable pension schemes rob people of life savings. They are made to suffer the grief of losing the security they had planned on and looked forward to in old age. A market-place ideology, which thinks of people as consumers, whether of health, education or of actual products, is especially bad for feelings incurred by loss or grief, for the market-place only values gain or profit. Loss is a failure.

Much of this market-place attitude has seeped into all grief, and all ideas about it. It has, as a Methodist minister said, 'devalued loss, and once loss is devalued, so is life. If losing a life is not so important, then neither is having one.' The minister is angered by what he sees as 'market values' creeping in everywhere: 'People these days have so little time for things like grieving. Basically it's considered less important than it used to be. There's tremendous pressure on people to pick themselves up, as if grief is a bad thing.'

He described how a parishioner, a man in his late forties with two young children, had almost had a nervous breakdown because of the pressure on him to 'get over' the death of his wife: 'There was all this lip-service about compassionate leave. When it boiled down to it, his employers wanted him back working as normal within ten days of his wife's death. Yet he had two children to make provisions for, and no relatives to help him. The poor man was on the verge of breaking down.'

The minister, who has himself lost a son, put forward a view expressed by many professional people who deal with grief regularly: 'When there's pressure on people, as there has been in the last decade or so, to spend, to get, to gain all the time, then everything gets seen in commercial terms. This is really unhealthy for people. It takes them away from what is "natural". Grief is a natural process. It is a natural response to loss. It is also an essential one, for if we don't grieve for our losses, we create trouble for ourselves.' He said that within grieving there are creative processes at work, which are vital to healing: 'If we don't grieve, we don't find that healing, and we don't repair ourselves.'

There is no doubt that not being able to accept loss is bad for us as individuals, and that our ability to be creative with loss is made more difficult when commercial gain is prized at the expense of human creativity. The diversity of human loss needs to be recognised in order that it be 'repaired', and therefore adjusted to. There is, for example, the necessary loss of children leaving home.

Jean, who is now in her mid-forties, spoke of her profound sense of loss when the second of her two daughters, like the first, left home for university. It was 1990 and it had been a bad year: her mother had died and her marriage had ended. One evening Jean found herself for the fourth night running sitting in the kitchen talking to the cat.

Bringing up the children had consumed her life, and being without them to look after 'left a huge hole': 'Kids take you over and I felt as if I'd been on a fast train for years and all of a sudden somebody'd set me down at a place I didn't recognise. I'd travelled all this way without seeing where I was going. I was completely lost, completely forlorn, like a stray kitten. There was this big empty space where daily life had been, you know, shouting at the kids, tidying up after them, nagging them about leaving phone messages, trying to keep them off the phone so I could get on it. Then there was nothing.'

Jean had given up teaching to have her children, and had returned to supply teaching when they went to secondary school. Then when her mother became ill, she gave up work altogether. After months of sitting at home talking to the cat, crying and feeling sorry for herself, she decided to embark on another career, as a counsellor. She had to wait to get on the course, but spent the time reading and studying in the local library. She believes 'life is a series of losses, as well as gains, which is where all the "personal greed" stuff which we're fed at the moment is such a lie. It doesn't prepare you for anything except winning. Life defeats you if personal greed is all that counts. You have to take the losses with the gains, otherwise you'd never do anything. You'd certainly never bring up kids.'

In common with a number of mothers, Jean spoke strongly about the 'necessary' grief, the 'necessary tears' of bringing up children, and of losing their childhoods: 'You bring up kids, and you lose them. You don't lose them for ever, but they return as different people. My friends tell me you gain adult friends from your children, but if you've brought them up to be independent, you can't rely on that either. Basically you've brought them up. Your job's over, and for a while you're redundant. I never thought I'd miss my kids the way I do. When they ring up they sound so "normal". They don't know that sometimes I've got a lump in my throat just hearing their voices . . . '

In her view, loss and gain are inextricably linked: 'Loss and gain go hand in hand. It's in all the old sayings. You can't have the rough without the smooth, you can't have the ups without the downs. But you can't have new gains unless you're prepared to lose old ground. Your kids can't be adults unless you let them go. The biggest cause of grief is not letting go.'

This was borne out by a bereavement counsellor at a hospice who thinks we handle loss badly because 'much of our value system is based upon having – and on getting': 'We don't know how to lose, how to let go of something. Yet we need to let go of so many things in so many ways in order to become adults, and if we are not educated towards this, we have a terribly difficult time.

'For example, we have to learn to live with regret, and with loss of opportunity, or the loss of a dream. It was a childhood dream of mine to be a ballet dancer, but I am not a ballet dancer. I might have spent the rest of my life grieving for that, but I didn't. Like so many people, I learned to live with my limitations. But some people find loss so frightening, it threatens them so much, that they never learn to live with it.

'My feeling is they should be given help to do this, to learn to cope with ordinary loss. But it's difficult for that to happen in a culture which only values gain.'

While there are obviously personal losses other than death and separation which cause us grief – loss of sight, loss of hearing, loss of a breast or a limb – there are also social griefs which beset us. In general, these are related to what used to be called our 'social consciences', our concern for people less fortunate than ourselves; like all universal griefs, they affect the lives of individual people.

A man in his late twenties is hurt by women's reactions to him as a man, and as a young, black man. As a central heating engineer, he goes into people's homes. 'It's usually women who are home, and their faces change when they open the door and they see you're black. They're frightened you're going to come into their homes and attack them. That causes me grief because it puts a big cloud over my job. I can't be cheerful when I'm working.

'I think grief happens when you get closed off, when you guard against the bad and you don't let in the good. It's like women on the phone. They're scared of weird phone calls or rapists so they answer the phone with fear in their voices, or like they're on a different planet. They keep the smile out of their voices on the phone, and you can't be cheerful then. You can't say: "Well, I'm going to make your day for you by fixing your central heating on time, and I'm not going to charge you too much . . . "' This man equated grief with lack of spontaneity, which he traced back to a feeling he had experienced following the death of his mother a few years earlier. Like the woman in chapter 1 who felt she was in a bubble, he too seemed to be cocooned after his mother's death: 'When my mother died, I didn't feel like smiling for a couple of months, and everyone else seemed a long way away, like I couldn't reach them, or they couldn't reach me. Like I was wrapped up in a blanket, or a shroud.' The lack of warmth in people's voices had a deadening effect on him, and stopped people from being spontaneous towards him: 'You don't get spontaneous things, and that's how grief feels.'

A number of older men found a problem with expressing grief. They thought they had to be strong and not 'give way' to their feelings of sorrow, at least not in public, or even, for some, with their wives. Without exception, the younger men interviewed – those in their late teens and twenties – felt differently about this. They did not consider it 'weak' for a man to express sorrow or to cry in public. They readily spoke of crying over the death of a parent, a sibling or a lover, and of crying openly. While they found this easier to do with female than with male friends, nevertheless close male friends were not excluded from the mourning process.

Younger men also drew a broad picture, and provided a wide-ranging account of what caused them grief. They gave unemployment as a direct cause, and cited examples where men they either knew or had heard of had attempted suicide because of it.

One man of eighteen said that the loss of his childhood had troubled him. He was the only child of an alcoholic mother, and had never met his father: 'I don't remember any happy times from being a child. My childhood is like a blank.' He especially missed pictures of himself as a child, baby pictures, and photographs of himself with 'Father Christmas'. Every once in a while he would go looking in the near-empty cupboards and drawers of the council flat he and his mother lived in. Even though he knew the pictures were not there, he would still look for them.

A number of people referred back to childhood to talk about grief, and to explain their first experience of it. A widow in her forties described her first experience of grief as being the ending of a book when she was sitting in an armchair reading at the age of about six or seven: 'The book was borrowed from the library. It was a Hans Christian Andersen story-book, which I devoured. It was quite thick and I became aware, after a while, that the fat bit of it was on the left side, and the pages on the right-hand side were running out. It was still a shock to get to the last page, and see writing on the left-hand side and a white blank piece of paper on the right. There was no more. The book was finished. For the rest of that day I experienced the most awful sense of loss – and alienation. I'm not sure whether I imagined part of me was still *in* the book, that I had lost a part of myself in it, but that was it, my first experience of a profound sense of loss.' The incident with the book gave her a feeling of being 'undone': 'For a while I couldn't put myself back together again.'

A woman in her late sixties who was born in India and came to Britain as a young bride spoke of a loss of nation as having informed all her adult life and having caused her a quiet but persistent kind of grieving: 'There's something in the air, in what you breathe, that is different in India, something I cannot explain. India was my mother. Now she is a stranger to me. I have lived all of my life here with part of me as a stranger in this country. It's something you never get over. It is like losing a part of yourself, something in your skin . . . '

How severely we experience loss of all kinds is affected by the human context in which we grieve. If we are surrounded by family and friends, we have a better chance of surviving grief than if we are friendless and without close human comfort. A woman in her sixties survived the death of her husband more than twenty years ago because both her mother and her son were there to support her. Her mother died within a few years of her husband, however, and her son died in an accident five years after that. For the last ten years or more she has led, like Frank, the man who carried a picture of his father in his wallet, a semi-reclusive life. A friend from her childhood years who still sees her on the odd occasion says: 'She coped quite well after her husband's death, and she even coped when her mother died, but when her son went . . . I remember her saying after her husband died that at least she had her family around her. After her son had gone she completely fell apart. She told me one day: "There's no one left to grieve with, no one who understands." I tried to tell her there were friends, like myself, and people in the village, but it wasn't enough. She'd suffered too much, really.'

A senior social worker, who has visited many families in grief, said that a good context for grieving was the extended family. She believes that the extended family, together with family doctors and neighbours, provides a good network for absorbing all of life's big events, from christenings, through weddings, to funerals. Like many professional people, she rued the loss of immediate access to uncles, aunts, grandparents, cousins, great-aunts and uncles – and even fathers – that the extended family provided. 'I'm not trying to suggest life was automatically wonderful when all those people were around in a family. What it offered was help with life's big events, with birth, with celebrations like weddings, and with death.

'It gave people a number of people to go to to talk, to cry or laugh with. You might not like one aunt, but you'd get on with another, and through her you'd learn to tolerate the first one. In an extended family you could usually find someone you got on with, who would help you. There were also, as I say, people around to mark the big events.

'The needs and feelings attached to those big events now have less avenues for outlet, less conduits. That's what the extended family did, provided a maze of outlets, like the roads on a map, for feelings to travel along. Now there are fewer roads carrying heavier traffic.' Elaborating on this last point, she added: 'It's as if there's more that we feel grief *for* these days, what with all the tragedy we hear about through the media. And at the same time there are fewer people to help us deal with it. That's why I think you've got the professionals coming in.'

A doctor who works part-time as a volunteer for the Medical Foundation for the Care of Victims of Torture deals with the grief of refugees: 'People who are refugees flee for their lives, and they've left everything behind them – their houses, jobs, family – and they arrive in this country with nothing, not even a language they can communicate in. In other words, they arrive with a huge burden of grief. They have lost their families, their homes, their jobs and their ability to be understood.'

He extends the context in which grief can be approached to include physical surroundings. For him, the space and environment of a garden is an important part of being able to allow and process grief. What he has done about this is to set up five large allotments to which he takes refugees so that they can begin to trust the sustaining and growing power of the land. Working alongside them, he helps refugees to grow vegetables, and to experience the common language of a garden. 'The allotments are a safe place for them. There are like-minded people, and people of many different races. A garden has its own universal language, and it offers them work, a sense of purpose, and results for that work. A garden also gives a context for trust, both because you trust the people you're with, and because you trust the soil to yield food if you plant in it and treat it right.'

He thinks the rest of us are understandably frightened by the overwhelming number of griefs suffered by some people: 'We are afraid to come too near people who have suffered terribly, partly because we're afraid we ourselves might break down, partly because it's so outside our carefully prepared boundaries. So given the weight of these problems, it becomes difficult to imagine you can do anything. And of course you can.'

The question of 'doing something' about loss turns us away from accepting grief, particularly other people's, for fear of being proved impotent. At least with our own, personal griefs we have to do something, even if only by accepting, eventually, that the loss has happened. With the grief of others we have a fear of being swamped, especially since, with war and famine, we feel helpless. There are so many losses that we know about these days. If we allowed ourselves to care about the victims of every war, every murder, every accident, how would we cope?

The answer to this seems to lie in the work of people who deal with grief on a wide scale, and on a daily basis. For what doctors, aid workers and other professionals do with the grief they confront through their daily work is, in a sense, simple: they do what they can. It is this 'doing' that empowers them and keeps at bay the sense of impotence which the rest of us feel overcome by. People involved in directly helping others – be they next door, down the road or in a different continent – use their grief. They teach people to plant crops in foreign lands, drive lorries of grain or feed children. They use their feelings of concern, outrage, fear, compassion, and therefore make themselves potent. They are more fully aware than most, usually, of the limit of this potency, which is not in any case the name they themselves would give their efforts. But it is what makes them able to continue.

I had often wondered how people could work with the amount of grief that aid workers, medics and people who look after the old, the sick or the mentally ill do. The answer given by many of them is that it helps them to be doing something, however little, rather than nothing. They are also helped by the fact that while general causes of grief belong in some measure to us all, they are not personal tragedies. But although personal and general griefs have different effects on us, the components are the same. What professionals do with the components is to turn them into action, and a fight for justice. That is what keeps them sane, and enables them to cope with grief on a huge scale.

As non-professionals, our own sense of justice comes into play during a tragedy. Most of us are said to behave at our best when faced with a sudden need to act or react to a crisis. When we are courageous, selfless or just deeply concerned, it is because we feel the grief of others. While we could not possibly become involved in every single violent death or unfair loss we heard of on the radio or TV, we nevertheless care. We would like peace, an end to the cruelty and relief from it. Most of us would feel happier in our beds at night if children were not starving, and if people were not being tortured and abused.

The purpose in saying this, and in discussing loss, lack and grief in a wide context, is to suggest that we, as individuals, experience the emotions involved in loss to some extent daily. The feelings so many of us encounter in general grief are, in fact, of the same nature as those in a personal grief, and vice versa. We therefore need not be as afraid of these feelings as we are. If we understand the prevalence of loss and of grief, its breadth and depth, it might be possible for us to view our own losses slightly differently – not as any less painful, but with the ability, as a doctor puts it, 'Not to add terror on top of fear.' She says: 'It is understandable to fear pain, of a physical or emotional kind, but ordinary fear is taken care of by the amount of things you have to do or learn after a loss. It's adding terror of the emotions involved in a loss on top of the emotions themselves that causes trauma. The vast majority of us are actually equipped to cope with loss. That's what we need to know. Loss of some kind or another is a daily event, and we have a tremendous wealth of experience to call on in dealing with it.'

That wealth of experience lies in our emotional responses which, during the course of accepting losses of all kinds, prepare us for big losses when they happen. And what is surprising when you analyse the emotions of grief is how honourable so many of them are. Anger is a highly honourable response to injustice; fear is an honourable response to loss and uncertainty; and guilt too is a principled and necessary first response. It can help us repair in the future that which cannot be put right in the past.

If we think of these emotions as friends rather than enemies, it is surprising how available they are to help rather than hinder us. When we ourselves are badly hurt, it is the passion and intensity of these emotions, as well as their substance, which we fear. We think they will drive us over the edge of what is endurable, when, in fact, their clamour is our potential saving. They are the protesters of our wounded selves. We have been hurt. They are outraged. They will resist, denounce and declaim on our behalf.

Like an angry army they come charging out to posture, protect and fight. They are courageous and noble because they will even protest against death, knowing they cannot win this battle, but they will still shout the odds and struggle against what cannot be changed. They do this for us, if you like, and give our minds the ammunition they need to begin the work of defending us. Without these emotions, without these passionate feelings accompanying a loss, deaths would go unremarked. And so would justice.

As it is, our passions surround us. Until our hurt selves are ready to stand up again, they encircle us as a form of camouflage. They are a hedge against a world outside which is impervious to our hurt, and which would have our losses pass unnoticed. Yet many of us view our emotions as dangerous, and have no idea they are on our side and not the 'enemy's'.

The real enemy is to deny that hurt of any kind exists, as one widower in his mid-fifties realises: 'It's the people who are not grieving who are causing the problems. Grief is natural. It picks you up in one place and puts you down in another. It's the journey of change, and of adjusting to change. It's people who can't do that journey who cause grief for the rest of us.'

It is indeed people and cultures who can behave only as if the world is a jolly playground where you swap a childhood fantasy for an adult one who cause untold grief. It is what I call the Disneyland syndrome, where life is viewed as a permanent party or whirl, and people who are sad – let alone grieving – are admonished or ostracised for being 'stick-in-the-muds' or 'spoilsports'. This is summed up in the old adage, 'Laugh and the world laughs with you, cry and you cry alone.' For a visiting American teacher, the phrase 'have a happy day' is the American equivalent of this; it makes her angry, especially since it has almost become an order: 'You have a happy day, now.'

She described the phrase as 'an insult to people's ordinary daily lives': 'I'd go as far as saying it's the single biggest cause of grief that we have the power to change. It's real grief if we have to address each other like that. I hate it when people say "have a happy day" to me when a kid's just been beaten up at school, and the world's in a mess.

'It's one of the great things about being in Europe, you don't hear it said. And you don't feel like committing violence fifty times a day. Back home I glare at people when they say it to me. Some of my friends do it too. The news is up there on the screen in the coffee shop and it's talking about shootings, and rape, and Somalia. And this guy – or woman – turns to you when you pay your check and says: 'Have a happy day." '

She made a sound through her teeth like ball-bearings being ground through a chainsaw and concluded: 'In the States we're very good at the smiles, and less good at the intimacy, the real stuff. If you're writing a book about grief, the global grief and personal grief go hand in hand. You can't smile or have a happy day all the time, treating real life as if it's Disneyworld, for Heaven's sake. But you could have much better quality of life for a lot more people if we all took more care of out hurt, and treated it more seriously.'

The way to care for that hurt is to accept loss and the strong emotions that can be connected with it, for if the emotions are felt or experienced, they can become part of one's own repertoire. Like a disciplined army, they can then be put to good use. People who have suffered or acknowledged individual griefs are better able to comprehend all griefs than those who have not. Being better able to understand them, they have more resources, more experience and more heartfelt feelings at their disposal to heal them.

Those people who have accepted the existence of loss and have 'processed' their grief have something which is missing from those who have not: a certain amount of humility and wisdom. There is no doubt that if you lose heavily, and are able to accept this and to learn to transform the feelings all loss produces into compassion and not revenge, then you have discovered something important and sustaining.

People who do not have an understanding of the balance of loss and gain, and who cannot therefore tolerate or accept loss, cause more grief. People who have the power to make important decisions – policy-makers, business leaders and politicians – have a bigger responsibility here, for in them rests much of the power to mitigate – or accelerate – the general and social grief which we all suffer from. It is even more important that people who make decisions for the rest of us recognise the balance of loss and gain, and do not try and package bad news as 'happy days'.

* * *

CHAPTER 6

Any Mountain High Enough

How both social and individual recognition are crucial to grief being accepted

For grief to be dealt with it has first of all to be recognised, both by those who are grieving and by those of us who are not. If grief is always seen as an accident which happens to others, then it will remain an isolating, lonely affair, and will not be brought into the realm of ordinary human experience. Grief also needs to be recognised on different levels, for an understanding of mourning, either our own or other people's, occurs at many different depths, from the cursory to the truly empathetic. Depending on our individual personality and on the nature and context of our relationships, we can understand deeply the nature of our own or anybody else's grieving or we can restrict our concern only to what is on the surface.

The danger in a surface view is that hidden hurts might be masked or covered up, and thus stop us from healing. People in interviews described this, how it is tempting to attend to superficial, practical matters at the expense of emotional ones.

Recognition is obviously a prerequisite for tending wounded feelings, but it must be a special kind of recognition. If a hurt is very deep, it will need to be fully recognised in order that it be 'mended'. For most of us, that recognition will need to come from others as well as from ourselves. This is necessary for our social benefit, so that we do not feel ostracised and 'odd'. Our loss needs to go on record.

It also matters to our personal, private well-being, for we are immensely helped by the knowledge that others truly empathise with us. When we are the only person bearing a grief or a loss, with no one else to understand it, it is easy for us to become ill. This happened to a woman who lost her husband after fifty years of marriage. He was considered by friends and neighbours to be a tyrant, and they therefore felt she was well rid of him.

Her daughter watched her mother go through untold grief because so many people would not recognise her loss; they thought she should be glad, not sorry, to be free at last from her husband's oppressive influence, of having to cook his meals exactly on time, and being at his beck and call. The daughter says: 'Mum knew Dad was bad-tempered as well as everyone else did. She'd lived with him, after all. She was OK after he died, with the funeral and all that. She was low, but managing. But she got terribly ill about six months later, and I'm sure it was because of people's attitudes. She said to me one day: "They don't treat me like other widows, you know. They take it out on *me*, as if his bad temper was my fault." '

The daughter thought, first of all, that neighbours in the small town where her mother had lived all her life had been deliberately unkind to her mother. It turned out it was not quite like this. What they had done, without meaning to, was to deny her mother her grief. Within far too short a time of the funeral they had made comments like 'Well, at least you can get out now' and 'It must be nice to have some freedom after all these years.' They had not appreciated – and, in fact, had failed to recognise – her loss. It was this she needed to have validated for what it was to her, not for what it looked like to them.

If nothing else, it was a loss of fifty years of marital habit, of tea making and drinking, of preparing food and eating, and of the company of another living person. For practically all of her adult life this woman had been married to the same man. There would have been intimacies and pleasures which kept her that way, as well as needs and conventions.

Not having our loss recognised is not an uncommon experience for any of us. It happens when a busy parent flushes a child's dead goldfish down the loo instead of reverently placing the body in a tissue-lined kitchen matchbox and burying it with due ceremony under the geranium; when a person is too busy with their own problems to understand the dashed or 'killed' hope of a new job a friend or partner has failed to get; or when we do not appreciate the loss of independence which many elderly people grieve over, and which makes some of them so sharp when we believe we are being helpful. They want recognition from us before they want help. They want to feel valued for the people they are before relinquishing themselves to often undignified assistance.

For grief to be recognised, the person or people experiencing it have to be known and understood. For if we do not recognise or understand a person, we will not see her or his grief properly. We might catch a glimpse of it, but we will not know its cause. The grief of non-recognition, of people not knowing who we are or who or what we have lost, is at the heart of all mourning. We can usually cope with a loss if someone else knows us well enough to validate it for us and releases us from the sense of isolation and estrangement that grief can bring. Were we confident of being known for ourselves, and not for the faces we put on for the outside world, we could bear our losses more easily because we would experience them from positions of security. We would feel less cut off by them.

The ordinary, daily grief of non-recognition was endured by a woman in her mid-fifties who spoke of how, roughly ten years ago, she started becoming invisible to half the human race. She is an attractive woman, but when her hair started to turn grey, she began to become 'invisible' in the eyes of men: 'You become a non-person. You go up to a man in the street to ask the way, or you start talking with a man at a cocktail party, and he looks through you as if you're not there. You realise what's going on. It's as if he can't see you. He has the label "old woman" pinned in front of his eyes, and whoever you are he can't see you through it.'

This woman explained that she did not enjoy being 'a non-person', for it took away her identity, and closed off a part of the world for her too. She added, wryly: 'It's like being buried long before your time.'

The grief of non-recognition usually stems from childhood and from an upbringing where parents, for a mixture of reasons – usually griefs of their own – cannot or will not accept us for who we are. Instead they want us to be different, particularly as we become adults, because they do not like the way we 'turned out'. Sometimes they would like us to remain as children whom they can continue to look after. Or, in other cases, they do not object to us as people, but they absolutely cannot get to grips with the work we do.

Many women spoke about a parent's unwillingness or inability to accept them as adults with public careers. An award-winning writer's mother was quite unable to accept that her daughter had achieved public success. She had wanted her to be something safe and simple like a secretary, something that the mother could understand, something she was not out of her depth with. So at a time when news of her second major award was being published the daughter received from her mother something which cut right into her celebration: a note containing a newspaper advertisement for a job she might like to apply for – as a secretary.

Another woman, Maggie, used to receive parcels for her birthday from her mother. They contained presents – things like gloves and hand-knitted woollen sweaters – that would have fitted a child of about nine or ten and were too small for the woman herself. Through these gifts her mother demonstrated that she had not accepted her daughter growing up at all and would relate to her only as a bright child and not as an accomplished adult.

Both these women experienced considerable grief from what amounted to denial of their true selves, their adult states, by their mothers. Maggie says: 'It was as if I was frozen at the age of nine or ten. Like some fairy story, my mother had waved a wand and kept me in ice. Of course I existed away from her as an adult woman, mainly by putting as big a distance between her and me as possible. But on my birthday, wherever I was, these parcels would find me out.'

By the time she was in her early thirties Maggie realised that her mother's deep-freeze treatment had affected her more extensively, and had pervaded her life more than she imagined, and she went into therapy, which ended three years ago: 'Part of the process of that work I did [in therapy] was to have to own up to my grief. I would not accept it to begin with. I thought it was my mother's problem, not mine. There then followed a painful time, which I would not like to have to repeat, where I suffered wave upon wave of all the feelings I had been sitting on, probably since I was ten. For that was the last time my mother recognised me.'

Not to be recognised for who we are as people, and not to be valued for what we have accomplished, either in personal or career terms, denies us the opportunity to be who we are. It denies us the opportunity to grow and to flourish. The act of recognition is necessary, both to attainment and to loss. We are able to achieve things and to be who we are because people recognise us as being our own individual selves and respond to us accordingly. In our losses, we grieve for losing someone or something recognisable to others as well as to ourselves.

Being a recognisable person – something we mainly take entirely for granted – is very important. When we suffer loss or grief, three kinds of recognition come into play: we ourselves have to recognise what we are going through; we have to feel that others understand too; and for that to happen they in turn must appreciate what is happening to us. It means 'the world' accepts us as an understandable entity in our own right and lets us, and our griefs, 'join the human race'.

The word 'understanding' could be used for the act, or the service, of recognising who a person is. I use the word 'service', for there is an element of giving or of devotion in true recognition or understanding. It takes time and commitment to know someone well. It is also necessary to lose or let go of some of your own dreams or fantasies about them.

Fantasies have to be relinquished if life is to continue, otherwise dreams do the opposite of what we would wish, and turn into nightmares. Maggie's mother had a fantasy that she could retain her daughter always as a child, and that she would never have to lose her daughter's childhood to adolescence and to womanhood. This turned out to be a nightmare in the short term for both mother and daughter. In the long term the daughter freed herself from her mother's fantasy, and in so doing left her mother alone with its consequences – estrangement. Maggie now visits her mother very little, and until her mother lets go of her dream that her daughter (her only child) will never grow up, her daughter stays away. So the mother's wish to keep a child for ever has lost her the person that child has become. By not letting go of the child she has lost the adult too.

Our need for recognition is, essentially, that we be understood for who we are, not for what people want us to be. We would like our own individual and unique hopes, losses, griefs and yearnings recorded in some way. This record, or recording process, usually takes place within relationships, whether they are close, casual or professional.

The standard excuse for our failures with other people's losses is that we all lead busy lives these days, and there is not the time to respond to the amount of bereavement of one kind or another we meet in people every day. This is only partly true, for an appropriate response to loss often takes no more time than an inappropriate one, as was demonstrated by an incident in a large teaching hospital. A young woman was sobbing, having just learned that the surgery she had undergone to enable her to have children had failed. She had been crying for about an hour or so when a nurse came round and said impatiently: 'Come, come, there are people worse off than you, you know.' It would be easy to make the excuse that the nurse was busy, but it would have taken no more time to say: 'I'm sorry your news is so bad.'

The nurse's response, of course, did not help the woman at all, and drove her instead deeper into grief. But it prompted a kind-hearted 'elder' lying in a bed in the corner to say: 'Take no notice of her, love. You cry as much as you like. I would if it was me.' As an aside to the others present she said: 'At least I've had my children. It must be terrible for her.'

Recognition of her grief was also initially missing from the mourning of a widow called Erika whose husband was a mountaineer. At the time of his death on a difficult climb her husband had their young son with him. The child was only six or seven years old, and was killed alongside his father.

In the newspaper articles which followed there were some scarcely veiled criticisms of both parents for allowing the boy to make this dangerous climb. There was, however, only one parent alive to read them and, to her credit, Erika became angered rather than cowed by what she saw in the papers. She was particularly furious about what the paper I was working for at the time had printed. It carried an insensitive report which suggested Erika was not even grieving over this tragedy. In high fury she phoned up the editor and gave him a giant slice of her mind. I was asked to visit her to try to smooth things over. To my surprise Erika agreed to let me in to talk. We then spent a few very fruitful hours together in which I learned about the difficult, solitary nature of her grief – and of her love for a husband who loved mountains.

Erika was a strong, proud woman who had managed to stay true to her husband's driving need to be a climber. This had been difficult enough, especially in a small community where life was hard, and where 'going off doing daft and dangerous things when he could be doing a proper job' was how the neighbours viewed her husband's pursuit of what he most loved. She had also had to accept that she came second to practically any mountain on earth, at least any mountain high enough.

What she had fought against for a number of years was her son's wish to climb. It was more than a wish, though, for he was, like his father, besotted with climbing and thought of little else. He was only happy when he was allowed out with his father, and if he was forbidden this and kept indoors or taken elsewhere, he became listless and even ill. Erika therefore felt she had as little choice in the matter of her son's love of mountains as she had in her husband's, but it was against her better judgement that her husband took their son out on more and more difficult climbs. The child, however, thrived on it, and his mother recalled his glowing eyes, energy and happiness when he was going out to or returning from mountains.

Erika believes the only way she could have stopped them going on the climb that eventually killed them both would have been to lock them up – for life. For if they were ever allowed to be free, they would both head straight for the nearest, highest and most dangerous peak. Father and son were inseparable, and seemed to derive complete happiness from each other's company and their shared passion. Her consolation was that they had died like that, doing what they loved together.

This was not as Erika's neighbours and family saw it. As in the case of the widow whose 'tyrant' husband died after fifty years of marriage, the speedily reached consensus was: 'She's been treated badly for years. She's well rid of him.' But added to this, in the neighbours' eyes, was the idea that Erika's supposed negligence might have had a hand in her son's death. In houses around her some people had the feeling she should have done more to save the boy from his father's wishes. In all of this they scarcely recognised, let alone validated, her grief. Within her own family she also received scant understanding from parents and a sister who had not wanted her to marry 'a man who loved mountains'.

Fortunately, Erika was a woman strong enough to have insult, or lack of recognition, added to injury, and to survive it. There were no tears on her part when we met, nor any bitterness – just a calm strength. The newspaper I worked for was not so strong. On returning to the office it was difficult to receive a pat on the back for my peace-making exercise, but find that nobody was interested in the real story. No one wanted me to write the 'real' article, the one that told her story as it was, or at least as I had understood it. It was now yesterday's news, and tomorrow's headlines were greedy for new dramas. But then, in a decade spent working for national newspapers and television, it was rarely possible, in my experience, for the might of the media to match or convey the strength and dignity of ordinary people. It seems to be a fact of life that the bigger the machinery or institution, the less it is able to express the truth of individual lives.

With the exception of remarkable people like Erika, ordinary men and women need to have their grief recognised as part of the healing process of recovering from grief. Part of the discharging of some of the pain is that we share it, or disperse it among others. This is accentuated in extraordinary circumstances as in the kinds of violent, unexpected or untimely deaths discussed in chapter 2. Where all these factors – violence, suddenness and untimeliness – come together is probably the point at which most newspaper headlines about grief are made. Many newspaper depictions of grief are of unusually severe griefs caused by exceptional losses. It is worth saying this because much of what we know of the world comes from the media, and the media's depiction of grief is perforce slanted towards exceptional griefs.

As a reporter working for newspapers I was often asked to 'cover' such exceptional losses, that is, to interview bereaved people in dramatic circumstances. At the time I never understood why people agreed to see me, or any other journalist. I did not comprehend why, with all the pain they were going through, they would add to it by repeating it yet again in telling the details of it to a complete stranger.

Since then I have come to appreciate the crucial part recognition plays in most griefs, and to see that as long as the stranger seems benign, the wish to have grief recognised by others will make many people talk. Talking is, in any case, a way of relieving the pressure, of offloading, in other words. What it achieves on top of this is recognition by another person of what you are going through. A bereavement counsellor described this in the following way: 'There are two questions I want the bereaved to answer for me: "What are you feeling?" and "What have you lost?"' These questions in themselves are acts of recognition in seeking to know how this particular grief has affected this particular person, and what this person's unique relationship was with whoever has left or died. She went on to say that there are two distinct stages in people's desire to talk out their grief. At one stage the wish is just to discharge emotion, and her job is to let them do that. At that stage, she believes, 'it wouldn't matter if you put them in front of a teddy bear. The need to talk is so great it all just comes pouring out.'

At the 'recognition stage', however, something quite different is required of her, and it is important that she is receptive to the difference: 'I would say everybody grieves totally differently. Every person is different, and every loss is different. And it is the uniqueness of that I have to recognise. Their story has to be unique to me for me to be of help to them, and I have to hear it for the first time. Once I stop listening properly to *their* story, once I let them see I think I know what they're going to say because I've heard someone else say it before, then I can't be of any use to them.' (This is not, of course, to suggest that different people's griefs do not have a great deal in common, for they do. But because we are individuals, the loss to us of an individual person needs to be recognised for what it is, an individual, unique loss.)

The reason it is often helpful to people to talk to newspapers and have the press make a big fuss is the need for public recognition for what is felt as a terrible loss. This happens in a variety of ways outside the media: in memorial services, in planting trees and in rituals like marking anniversaries. A couple who had lost a son in his twenties spoke of one of their son's friends' wish for 'big recognition' of the loss they were all suffering. In common with many people who experience untimely losses, their son's friends had 'done' something by setting up a charity in his name. After a year had gone by they had accumulated a certain amount of money through fund-raising events and wanted to know how best to use this in their son's name, and for the common good. The charity organisers, consisting of the parents and friends, met. Barbara, the dead man's mother, told the story of what happened at this meeting: 'The first time we discussed what to do about the money I saw Brian was fidgeting. We were sitting in the dining room. He was in the carver chair at the end of the table, and his bottom was wriggling on the chair, and his arms were fidgeting. And I said: "What do *you* want?" And he said first of all he didn't know what he wanted done with the money. But he kept on fidgeting and I said: "Come on, you're not happy. You're fidgeting away. Tell us what you want." Then he said: "I know what I want in my heart. I'll tell you what I want. I want lights in the sky all over London, and I want them to spell out . . . "' And here he said his dead friend's full name.

Grief is not always or necessarily a private affair. It might be relatively private in needing only a witness or two, rather than many, and it may be that the recognition or attention of the witness is all the more important because of that. A woman in her thirties described one such witness, someone who helped her recover from an attempted rape fifteen years ago. The incident had taken place on a late-night tube which travelled through a number of stations without stopping. Although brief, the attack was severe enough that the woman's neck and legs were scratched and bleeding. She and her assailant were alone in the compartment, and as the train drew into the next station, the man ran off. The woman attempted to get help from two ticket collectors, one female, who both laughed at her and refused her request to call the police. The man had also masturbated over the woman's clothes, which added considerably to her distress.

At the time she shared a flat with several people: 'one of whom was a gay man called Dan. Those were the days when things were quite free and easy, and there were always loads of people staying. That night I ran home, crying and sobbing, and the only person in at the flat was Dan. I told him what had happened, and he was absolutely wonderful.' She explained that he not only recognised her distress, but immediately became very angry on her account, as if he, himself, had been injured. 'First of all, he was furious on my behalf, which, although I didn't realise it, was exactly what I needed. "How dare he?" he shouted. "How dare he do that to you?"

'Then he picked me up – he was much taller than me – and carried me into the bathroom. There he took off all my clothes, and dumped them as if they were rubbish, into the corner. I'm not sure I ever saw them again. I had long hair at the time, and he gave me a bath from top to toe, hair and all. And all the time he kept on bringing me tissues and wiping my nose and talking to me. Then he wrapped me in a huge towel, sat me on his knee and cuddled me in front of the fire. I cried and cried and cried, and he just kept on rocking me, and stroking my hair, and saying: "There, there."'

This woman feels she was healed by her flatmate's actions, and that a vital component of that healing was his instant recognition of her pain – and therefore of the needs she had arising from it: 'One of the best things he did for me was to be angry *for* me. And he didn't ask a single question, then or afterwards. He didn't ask if I wanted the police called, which I didn't by that time, it was too late. And although I would never have been able to ask for what he did, he did exactly what I needed. He made me clean again.'

A psychotherapist who works a great deal with people suffering from the after-effects of trauma said of the importance of other people's intervention on our behalf: 'A component of grief is almost totally dependent on other people – and that is your passage back into the world again after a trauma or a loss has happened. If people don't believe you've suffered a loss, then they can't or won't acknowledge your grief, and they won't let you back into company again. If they can't fathom what it is you're grieving for, they just won't let you back in. They'll ostracise you.

'People can be very uncompromising in the face of something they don't understand or can't relate to. This is where recognition, and communication, is so important. I think a lot of us don't speak about our griefs because we are afraid of rejection. We are afraid people will be indifferent to them. It's a risk we have to take, though, because if we don't, we put at risk future relationships and future happiness.'

It would be true to say that all good relationships are based on recognition – as is the key to dealing with the grief which comes from their endings. If the grief of the loss of a relationship is not accepted, then 'loose ends' lie around to trip us up in the next relationship. The recognition, however, needs to be more than superficial. It needs to be truthful, for there is no point in tending a few cuts and bruises if the real problem is a broken heart.

* * *

CHAPTER 7

Plastic Hearts on the Fridge

Why truthfulness is also crucial – and not always easy

When we recognise a grief of our own, we present it to other people so that they can help us with it. Quite simply, we tell them we have lost someone important to us. Implicit in this telling is a question about how truthfully we represent our loss, and how we portray the past. Either we speak the truth when we tell other people of our losses, or we embroider our stories. We can, in fact, misrepresent them entirely, by suggesting, for example, that we have lost a 'wonderful' husband or wife when the truth is that the marriage was a war-zone.

The importance of being aware of the full truth of an individual grief was highlighted by a bereavement counsellor working in a community health centre. She told of how she visited an elderly widower whose wife of almost fifty years had died six months previously. He had rung the health centre to ask for some assistance because he was not coping very well. But it was not grief over the loss of his wife herself that was really troubling him. The counsellor arrived to find, as she put it, 'plastic hearts on the fridge and an angry man'. 'Basically he was missing all the things his wife did for him – but not his wife. He was in a right old stew about the fact that his shirts weren't the way he wanted them, and he couldn't find things, and he wasn't eating properly. What he actually wanted was practical help.'

The counsellor arranged some practical assistance in the form of a home help, but since the man was still relatively active, there were things he simply had to learn to do. When she visited him again, his anger was more evident: 'He swore at his dead wife, asked why she had to be spiteful and leave him. When I left, I suggested to him that he wasn't missing his wife for herself, but only for the domestic chores she did.'

Over the next couple of months the counsellor visited this client a number of times, and he began to improve. 'I knew things were getting better when the hearts came down off the fridge. He said he didn't like all the sentimental nonsense of the hearts anyway, but his wife did, which is why he'd left them up. The next time I visited he explained she was a good woman, but their marriage had been a disappointment. Then I suggested to him that he could grieve for *that*, his disappointment . . .'

In asking the surviving husband to grieve truthfully, for his disappointment and not for a sentimental image of either his late wife or their marriage, the counsellor was hoping to achieve two things. First, she hoped that understanding his disappointment might enable the man to have some compassion for himself. Instead of grieving in a sentimental way, which would keep him in the past, he might grieve in a truthful way, and step into the future. In other words, in sorrowing genuinely over disappointment in his past, he would find the means to avoid bringing himself any more disappointment. Secondly, the counsellor was hoping the man would have the prospect of living with his wife in his memory as a real person rather than a sentimentalised one. Rather than carrying around the trappings of all those plastic hearts, he might be able to see her for who she really was, and therefore do both her and himself justice. He might, therefore, truly lay her to rest. This, in turn, would help him to live in the present in a stronger, more honest way.

It is tempting for some of us to reinvent a relationship after a death because we do not wish to accept or to believe the past. Where it has been unhappy, we would like it to have been different, and we would like to show ourselves and our relationships in a better, rosier light. Our belief that it is 'wrong' to mourn a bad relationship also comes into play here. More to the point, as was shown in the last chapter, we fear other people will not allow us our fair share of compassion over the loss of a difficult relationship. We think we will only gain other people's sympathy if we say we have lost something good.

In fact, close friends will validate the loss of something 'bad', as will professionals, for they will understand that the process of grieving an unhappy relationship involves the mourner in an extra journey. He or she must face not only the grief itself, but also the difficult task of accepting his or her own collusion in a poor marriage or partnership. Beset by grief anyway, this can leave people further weakened as they come to terms with their own inadequacies.

Our wish not to believe in the truth of the past and to tamper with that truth is exacerbated by bad relationships. They ill prepare us for the courage to face an ultimate truth: however much we have complained about a poor relationship, we stay in it, in the main, from fear of loneliness. So when a bad relationship ends, our worse nightmares come to pass. We are left alone, as we always feared we would be, and how are we to grieve? People who know how bad things were will surely reject our tears.

The loss of a bad relationship is consequently more difficult to recover from than the loss of a good one. It may require more compassion and understanding from us, not less. It certainly requires more work. For within bad relationships we have developed and consolidated bad habits. We have been badly treated, and have often lost confidence in ourselves as people who can be independent and courageous. We have lost sight of our lovable selves, and have therefore become clumsy about finding love and affection. We face the future with little hope that there will be good life after grief.

When we are feeling inconsolable and want sympathy, there is a strong temptation to believe that we can make of the past what we want. We can create for ourselves some hope for the future by reinventing the past along more favourable, optimistic lines. And since the dead are not here to dispute this dishonesty, the living sometimes feel we can 'get away with it'. The fact is, we cannot. Dressing up a past relationship in ornaments on the fridge, or seeing it through rose-tinted spectacles, backfires. Other people recognise the lie quite intuitively, even when they are strangers to our lives.

Sheila, a widow in her sixties, spoke of this when she told of meeting another widow on holiday. Sheila's husband had died about eighteen months earlier and the other woman's husband had been dead only a few months. The women were sitting next to each other on the plane taking them to Jersey, and when Sheila heard of her companion's plight, she suggested they had dinner together at the hotel that night: 'Since her husband had only recently died, I felt real compassion for her. It's such a horrible feeling, a death, and you really don't know at the time how you're going to get over it.'

During dinner it became clear to Sheila that the woman she was dining with was 'a dead weight' because she was not telling the truth about her marriage: 'You just know if someone has had a good relationship. You just do. And she was pretending their relationship had been marvellous, and it obviously hadn't been. All this was dragging her down because it's actually simpler to tell the truth. She was contradicting herself, and going red in the face, and getting in a real state.

'So after a bit I leaned over, put my hand on hers and said: "Look, it's all right. You don't have to pretend with me. Very few marriages are perfect. Mine certainly wasn't." And she reacted like a scalded cat.'

Sheila did not spend any more time alone with her dinner companion, even though she would have been pleased to do so: 'I glimpsed her from time to time and felt really sorry for her. She was like an outcast in the group. Yet if she'd been honest, I'm sure most of us would have responded to that, and she would have got some comfort.'

For some people the barely recognised feeling that you are not allowed to grieve for someone if they are not 'nice' gets in the way of honesty. 'Altering' a person's character after they have died prevents the living from grieving for something in a truly honest way – their loss of a relationship. Whether or not the relationship has been a good one is not initially what most matters. What is important is that something which has gone on for a long time has been lost. It does not have to have been 'good' for the loss of it to cause pain. But grieving has to be honest for the sense of loss to heal. If it is not, the person remaining will be stuck in an idealised and invented version of the old relationship, unable to 'escape'.

One psychotherapist believes that if 'people reinvent the past, they're stuck with the invention': 'It's important for people to grieve what they have truthfully lost, and to do that in their own way. In a marriage that has not been passionate, for example, it would be damaging to pretend it had been. But a lot of passion could be involved in grieving for, say, the *habit* of that marriage. If a person has lost something they've been used to, even if what they had is not very satisfactory, it was still theirs, and took up a lot of their time and commitment. So even a minimally satisfying relationship will be grieved for.'

Kathy, now in her late thirties, spoke of this in relation to her mother's behaviour after the death of her father three years ago. Her parents had had what she described as 'a bickering marriage', and she had imagined that after her father's death her mother would come into her own. This was not, initially, the case. Kathy said: 'It took me a long time to understand the terror she was experiencing. It wasn't what I'd call grief, but the death of my father caused my mother to be terrified, and this became part of her grieving process.

'She was perfectly capable while he was alive, and I tried to console her with this, until I realised it wasn't where the problem lay.' The problem lay in the mother's dependence on her dead husband: 'They were terrifyingly dependent on each other. They didn't have friends, and very few people called at the house, so they just clung to each other. And although my mother was capable in a practical sense, her terror was that without my father she wouldn't survive emotionally.'

As well as the grief for an emotional entanglement – even, or perhaps especially, a bad one – further grief arises if we start to embellish the past. The psychotherapist referred to this as causing grief to our 'moral selves': 'It's damaging to reinvent the nature of a person or a relationship afterwards, for we all have an impetus to be truthful. We might not consciously realise this, but we do. It's part of our moral centre, part of the way most of us are brought up. We have a sense of what's right or wrong, what's truthful or not, and if we "offend" that, we suffer. We cause ourselves more grief.'

It seems that someone who reinvents the nature of a dead person suffers two griefs. They suffer the loss of someone they have become dependent on; and they suffer the loss of the potential to use people's words and small kindnesses to form new bonds and friendships, and gradually to experience the feeling that life can be hopeful again. If we lie about whom, or what, we have lost, people's words to us will be influenced by those lies. The words are, after all, offered as responses to what we say. They relate to our words, and if our words are untruthful, other people's do not get at the truth of our loss, and therefore cannot help us move forward.

The bereaved are held back in another way if they succumb to reinvention, for it drains their own ability to be creative. It prevents them from forming new friendships which are based on solid, believable ground, and it prevents them from bringing about change in themselves. A person cannot become emotionally capable and independent after the death of a partner unless he or she realises that changes must take place. Without truth recovery is blocked.

The need to be remembered truthfully, and not to be sentimentalised, was something David, a man in his early forties, spoke about in relation to another aspect of recovery from grief, the way we say goodbye through services of burial or cremation. The woman he lived with, Dee, had died only a few months previously, and he spoke of the importance, in her mind, of being truthful about the dead as well as the living. Before she died Dee had told David of her shock at an incident during her father's funeral when she was fourteen. A vicar whom her father had never met had spoken copious and, to her ears, insincere words about her father. The funeral was spoiled for her because of this, and she had decided, almost there and then, that her own funeral would be different. David recalls: 'She was so disgusted at this oily vicar saying wonderful things about her father when he'd never set eyes on him when he was alive that she told me before she died she didn't want anything of the sort to happen to her. Dee didn't want anyone to talk over her dead body who didn't know her as a living person. And she got her way. The people who spoke at her funeral service knew her and loved her. She left money in her will for us all to celebrate, and we drank fifty bottles of champagne in the pub next door.'

David made sure he got his way over another part of the funeral arrangements. He kept Dee's body in the house until she was cremated, going back to the old convention whereby after a death a person was 'laid out' in the front parlour. 'I wouldn't let the funeral directors take her away and basically stick her in a fridge. That's the truth of what happens there. I let them come in and do what they had to do, but I said: "No embalming, no extra preparation. I want her to be simple, and the person she was."' There was one small concession. Dee had died of cancer, and had lost most of her hair through chemotherapy. She and David had bought her a wig, which she had grown fond of wearing, and which was far more luxurious than her own hair, even at its best. David insisted 'she wear that wig which we'd gone out to get for her together, and which she loved'.

A woman in her late forties, Rachel, whose father died after a short illness when he was in his seventies, also spoke of the importance of truth at the burial service. She had not got on with her father, and felt that he had been unkind to her mother, herself and her sister: he was 'a bad-tempered, opinionated man whom it was very difficult to be with'. He did not seem interested in his five grandchildren, but only in keeping his wife to himself. Rachel admits: 'In a way I was dreading him dying, because I knew I'd have very mixed feelings. I'd been angry with him practically all my life. He was the stumbling block in family outings, and he stood in the way of my sister and I seeing as much as we wanted of our mother.'

She nevertheless wept when her father died, and realised she wanted to honour his life, but not in an untruthful way. 'My mum, my sister and I sat down, and we began to write on a piece of paper the things that typified Dad, like the fact that he always wanted Sunday lunch on time, and that he was careful with money, that he'd only make short phone calls, and tell us off if we spent too long on the phone, even though it wasn't his phone bill and we were grown-ups . . . the list went on.' By the time the three of them had finished, the two grown-up daughters were weeping hard. One turned to hold the other and said: 'You know what he was, don't you? He was a frightened man.'

Rachel now thinks there was a good deal of truth in that: 'It wasn't until we began to write it down that we saw it. Dad was frightened. It doesn't mean he still wasn't nasty and difficult, but I felt as if we'd found a reason for it.' What the sisters then did to honour their father, and their discovery of him after his death, was to write, with their mother, their own portrayal of their father to be read out when he was cremated.

Rachel enjoyed her father's funeral and believes many things were laid to rest that day: 'What we had written were the ordinary things about Dad, the funny things, like he'd only put two cups of water in the kettle. And everyone else there, all the relatives, recognised these things and said how lovely it was. Much better than if the vicar had said something about a man he'd never met.

'I feel quite peaceful since he's died because what we did at his funeral was honest. It wasn't hypocritical. We didn't try to pretend he was the most marvellous father and husband in the world, because he wasn't. But he was *our* father, and we said that.'

There is, in fact, as much hypocrisy surrounding loss and grieving as there is in any other aspect of life. Another man described his anger over the attitude of an uncle he and his sister call Uncle Death: 'He only came when someone was dying, and he loved it. He really loved a death. But he never came to see the living. If people were alive and well, he wouldn't travel a hundred yards to see them. He was a real funeral-monger, and I couldn't stand the sight of him.

'I remember when our Aunty May was dying. She was a dear old lady, and we'd visited her over the years and done her shopping and made her cups of tea. On her deathbed in swarms Uncle Death, all in black, and sits himself beside her. He hasn't seen her for years, but there he is by the side of the bed polishing off his tea and sandwiches we've made for him and holding Aunty May's hand. He turns to us, his face positively beaming, and says: "Look, she's slipping away now. Look at those roses in her cheeks." And my sister had to stop me going over to the bed and wringing his neck for him.'

This man's only other sibling, a brother, was killed at the age of twenty-nine in a car crash, and he spoke of something else in connection with his objection to the 'falseness' which he finds disturbing about some people's reactions to grief: 'When my brother was killed, someone phoned to give me the news. I can't remember who it was now. I was married at the time, although the marriage broke up quite soon afterwards. I didn't say anything to my then wife. I went outside straight away, got in the car and drove slowly round some country lanes, just looking around me. I stopped a few times, just looking over the countryside. I have no idea what I was thinking about.'

When he got back to the house about an hour later, his wife was furious. 'She wanted to know what I'd been doing driving round by myself. And I remember her saying: "It's not normal. It's not what people do, driving off by themselves." And I shouted back at her: "It's what *I* do. It's not like watching your table manners, you know. You don't have to do it in a certain way. This is *my* way of doing it." '

The truth of recognising grief and loss extends far beyond the 'how to mourn' conventions. Both this man and his brother loved fast cars, so for him to have gone off alone in his own car was an understandable response to his brother's death. But not in his wife's eyes. He said: 'She was shouting at me: "People talk, that's what they do. They don't drive off without saying a word. You'll have to talk it out, you know." I remember thinking, not with you, I won't.'

There turned out to be a deeper significance in this, for the marriage split up shortly afterwards. Loss and grief put tremendous strain on relationships, and it is only the strongest that survive them. This goes against the idealised view that marriage or long-term partnership in themselves provide support during a time of severe loss. In reality they do so only if they are already sustaining and good; if they are poor, then the loss of a job or a hope, of a parent or a child, will only add to the strain.

Most of us do not have a profound understanding either of grief itself or of relationships. We come to our first severe loss as we come to our first important relationship, relatively unprepared. A number of people spoke of this sense of not being forewarned. They all felt the same thing, that relationships themselves, and the grief caused through their loss, should be something we generally know more about. They also thought that schools were a good place for this to begin, especially during teenage years. They wanted there to be an introduction to ideas and feelings about grief when people were young.

A man who lost both his parents when he was a child feels particularly strongly about this. As a result of his treatment then he sees the whole world as deficient and mendacious in its portrayal of loss. He thinks emotions are 'laundered' because people are more comfortable that way. So expediency replaces truth, and a cliché like 'you're young, you'll get over it' replaces real care for a child's grief.

In his own case, people's poor handling of the grief he experienced when he was still in his teens is something he keenly remembers and still sees happening to other people. 'You're stopped from having the big emotions because people might not be able to handle those, so you're told to "hush" and "keep quiet now" and "brush things under the carpet". You get to play sport because people, teachers, other adults, think that will be good for you. In fact, it's the only way they know how to handle grief in an adolescent boy.'

He recalls being sent out to play by his grandparents if he got upset, 'as if physical exercise would solve the problem of losing a mother and a father'. As an adult he views all this as so much avoidance. Even accepting, as he can now, that his grandparents were also grief-stricken, he sees it as our general inability to handle the depth and breadth of our own or anyone else's emotional world: 'So what you're left with is the small emotions showing, the ones that aren't going to trouble anybody, and the large ones remain submerged like a big volcano ready to erupt.

'It doesn't give anyone a chance when death and loss are washed out of our society the way they are. It doesn't give anyone the opportunity to grieve, or to live properly. If you can't grieve, for Heaven's sake, how can you live a real life? How can you make anything better for the next generation if you can't talk about loss, if all you know about is so-called acquisition?'

In his opinion, the pressure to become consumers in a society which values wealth and consumption more than important feelings leads us to pay too little attention to grief, and therefore to lie about it: 'It's a dreadful lie to pretend that living is about getting things and consuming all the time. It takes away from all of us our ability to grieve naturally, if you like, to know and understand the feeling of loss and not to be afraid or overwhelmed by it. Of course loss is a part of what happens to all of us every day. Most of the time we don't think about it, but there are bits we need to consider in order to understand ourselves. And these are the bits that make us understand other people as well, that give us our compassion.

'What I'm really trying to get at is variety. There is no one character to loss or grief. Your grief isn't mine, but I can help you with your grief if I know what mine looks like, if I know what it consists of, or what shape it is. But if no one looks at these things, how can we see them?'

The cost of not knowing the true nature of grief, and of lying about its character and prevalence, is high for those undergoing loss, and for those who will undergo it tomorrow or the next day. A number of people asked if I would do themselves and other people a favour by writing the truth about grief, and by presenting it and the feelings it produces in all its complexity. They wanted it given its true colours, as something to be understood, not washed down the drain. But in coming to this understanding of grief, the truth of it can seem like a Russian doll, where lifting off one layer reveals another, and then yet another.

A counsellor called Nichola feels that looking at grief seems to have presented her with never-ending layers of loss, each one concealing another. The first loss is connected with her mother, whose minor stroke eighteen months ago was followed by the trauma of having her leg amputated. She has struggled, at the age of seventy-one, to learn to use an artificial limb, but finds it extremely difficult and frustrating. Her alternative, however, is to spend the rest of her life in a wheelchair. Nichola says: 'She's lost her whole lifestyle. Bowls was her activity. She was there at the club every day, and that's where she socialised and got her exercise. She suddenly finds herself in a completely different situation, which she hasn't prepared for, and just experiences as devastating loss – with no gains. And the element of anger that's always there in a loss, it's hard for her to know who to be angry at. How are you angry with doctors who save your life? She lives on her own, and now it's difficult for her to get around. Who can she be angry with?'

But within her mother's loss, Nichola has discovered a loss of her own, the loss of her energetic, capable mother: 'I've had a struggle dealing with my own loss, the loss of my healthy, happy mother, who came up and baby-sat sometimes at weekends and helped with the children. She has vanished, and instead there is somebody who needs me, who is miserable instead of cheerful, and makes demands of me whether she wants to or not.'

Because of this Nichola finds it difficult to hear about her mother's pain, and has suggested her mother see a counsellor, someone other than her daughter. But her mother, being a woman who is not used to confiding in strangers, has resisted. This is complicated by the fact that mother and daughter live 250 miles away from each other. 'A few weeks ago she rang to say she was very depressed, and I said: "I'll come down and see you this weekend." I was very upset by how depressed she was feeling, and I told her how upset I was too, and I started to cry, and she started to cry, and she was apologising, and I said: "Please don't, because I need to cry about this too because it's awful . . . " While I want her to express her feelings, I find it really hard to bear, which is why I want her to talk to somebody else . . . '

Herein lies the kernel of what troubles Nichola: although she is used to being a counsellor for other people and, in fact, trains counsellors, she does not want to counsel her own mother. It is partly a professional decision, but also one based on the deeper truth of what she sees inside herself. For her mother's loss has, for the first time, revealed in Nichola a fear of ageing: 'I've always had this view about ageing being a mixed thing which involves some losses, but also some gains, and I haven't been afraid of "growing old". Seeing what's happened to my mum has thrown my confidence about ageing and I find that hard as well. I've lost that feeling of security about it, and I don't know when it's going to return, or if it will.'

Being prepared to accept that truth has, however, enabled Nichola to cope with her own children's fears about their grandmother: 'We bring up our children to be truthful, but it wasn't until I faced this myself that I realised how untruthful we are about loss. I've told them now that perhaps their grandmother won't get better, and maybe if I hadn't paid attention to my own experience, I might have tried to gloss it over for them. As it is, they seem to have accepted the status quo. And it's made them a bit more considerate towards her.'

When looking at deeper issues of loss and grief, a man in his mid-forties who has just gone through a divorce said he felt the subject was important enough to be on the school curriculum: 'People don't tell you the truth about it because they're afraid of scaring you. But it's only the truth that can prepare you for it, and some kind of knowledge that other people suffer this too, so you're not the only one. As it is, people cover it up, and cause a lot of misery through that.

'I'd say there is a need for people to be educated about it. There needs to be education of people to understand what is happening to them, and if they understand, they can cope so much better. Some people can spend the rest of their lives trying to recover from a loss or a grief because they were never prepared for it.'

Being prepared for grief, knowing the truth about it, was something that troubled a woman called Oona in quite a different way. An ex-lover of hers was dying. It was obvious, she says, that he was not the marrying kind, and since that had become clear to her, they had developed a very special friendship over a period of fifteen years. They lived in different countries, and when she had seen him six months previously he had looked fit and well and had mentioned nothing about being ill.

Oona was shocked to hear one day from a mutual friend that her ex-lover was dying. She immediately flew to Paris to visit him, and was even more shocked to find out that her friend was not prepared to face the truth of his dying. He would talk about everything except the cancer which was killing him, and which meant he had no more than six months to live. He behaved as if he would get better at any moment, and tried to make plans with Oona for a walking holiday the following spring to revisit one of their favourite haunts. He behaved, in other words, as if his illness was temporary rather than fatal. Oona knew he had been told the truth: 'He knew what the score was, and I experienced the most awful torment about what to do or say. It also faced me with a terrible dilemma. The torment was that I felt he was making a lie out of his own death, and I hated to see that. When we spoke, I didn't know what to say to him. We'd had a very truthful relationship, and he'd been very good to me, and he was dying and I couldn't relate to what he was doing about that. My dilemma was what to do about it all. I felt if anyone was going to get him to face up to the truth, it would be me, but . . . '

Oona's 'but' was a quandary between one truth and another. It was true her friend was dying and had not faced up to it. But was it not also true, she thought, that he had the right to be allowed to die in his own way? He had led a life in which he valued honesty, and whatever reasons he had for refusing to talk about his death she felt she had to respect his wish. With some reluctance, therefore, she put aside any thought, as she described it, of 'trying to force him to do something he clearly didn't want to'.

It was not until a few days before her friend died, when she visited him for the last time, that Oona discovered the other possible truth underlying his resistance. As she tearfully said her last words to him, aware that she would never see him again, her friend surprised her by refusing to say goodbye to her. As she said 'goodbye' to him, he shook his head fiercely and whispered: 'Never goodbye.' Oona cried all the way to the airport. 'I felt completely helpless. I'd had to say goodbye to *him*, but it seemed he'd refused to say goodbye to me.

'It wasn't until we were airborne and I was sitting with my face to the window, tears rolling down my cheek, that I remembered something. Years previously he'd said to me once when I told him I'd been feeling lonely that I must never feel lonely while he was alive. He said that while he was alive I would always be cared about, wherever I was, and however far apart we were. He said it as a kind of oath or promise. At the time I'd thought it was very sweet of him, and typical of his kind of romantic gesture. I'll never know, of course, but it occurred to me, flying back into London, that that's why he wouldn't say goodbye to me. He didn't want to break his word.'

The individual character of any loss can only be fully assessed by the person who has experienced it. Once that is done, it will be conveyed to others. How they recognise it will depend on the description given, and whether or not it is accepted as an honest grief.

What has been said in this chapter is that honesty about the large and complicated feelings produced by grief is not always encouraged in an adult world which values circumspection more than truth. It is not therefore always within the power of any one individual to be truthful about the deep nature of a grief – but it is up to all of us.

We can, in other words, help each other to understand our griefs more truthfully and, in doing so, learn to work with them rather than against them. A way forward through grief is to allow mourning its true journey and nurture circumstances which do the same. Our losses can then become creative parts of our lives rather than dark secrets which we fear will eventually find us out.

* * *

CHAPTER 8

Stopping the Clock

Time with a capital T plays a large part in mourning. The ability of unresolved loss to play unpleasant tricks with time

Time plays tricks with us when we mourn. One minute it is racing along, and the next it has stopped. One day a person is with us, and the next their time has run out. They are gone; we are stranded; and as we look around, the world appears flat and grief seems endless.

The 'truth' of the role time plays in long-term relationships is important to grasp. It is both friend and enemy, both healer and implacable foe. It flies when we are in love and appears to stand still during grief. When a relationship ends, time seems to consist of so many concrete-grey hours, days, weeks – horizons, or long bridge-spans, full of them. Yet the cliché 'time will heal' is said to so many people in grief at the very moment when time seems to be the enemy. It has finished for the person who is dead, or for the relationship that has been abandoned. It hangs heavily on those left behind, or can seem, temporarily, like 'a life sentence', as one person put it.

Terry was widowed three years ago after twenty-six years of marriage. He believes that of all the things said in the name of comforting those who are grieving, one of the most vexing is the phrase 'time will heal'. 'I thought of writing a handbook of what not to do when people die. The worst thing ever told you is "time will heal".' The intensity of his feelings in the weeks and months following his wife's death was such that platitudes like this further wounded and angered him. 'Generally well-meaning people said that to me – "time will heal" – and that's the last thing you want to hear. Your world is at an end. It's stopped. The phrase goes against everything you're experiencing. When someone you love dies, there is no time and there is no future. To actually believe in a future at that time is like abolishing death. My wife's future had gone. She had no future and, for a while, neither did I.'

Like the mother who talked to the toys and who had wished to remain face down over her daughter's coffin (see chapter 3), some people make an important journey after a death. For death itself brings up the whole stark question of past and future – by stopping the future of the person who has died. Death is the end of time for one person, and yet time continues for others. The living person has then to make a journey, not from birth to death, but from death to birth. The living, or the people 'left behind', have to find ways of moving from the coffin out into the world again – a world where there is a future.

Terry had a particularly difficult time in the early stages of grieving because he had lost so much. He and his wife had had a particularly close relationship, having met as students, and they had spent most of their adult lives in each other's company. Their jobs, in higher education, had meant they had travelled the world together, and they shared common political interests and worked for a number of charities. They had one child, who was at university when his mother died. In Terry's opinion: ' "Time will heal" is like an insult. It's just so crass. People who say it mean well, and of course it's true, time does heal eventually. But when that's being said to you, usually in the early stages of grieving, when you're at your worst, it's a kind of *non sequitur*. It doesn't mean anything because your world has just ended, and if your world has just ended, time has no point. The past has gone and there is no future. That's what it feels like, or that's what it felt like to me.'

He also thinks that in the early stages of grief clichés generally were some of the worst things he had to face because the intensity of his feelings made them seem like nonsense. Although he is 'not the suicidal type', and has remarried, he clearly remembers, for a while, not wanting a future: 'I did not want time to heal because at the beginning that would have meant getting over her death, and I didn't want that. I only wanted her back. I didn't want a new life, or any life that involved being without her. And to accept that you're going to get better involves leaving the past behind. I didn't want to leave her behind, and I didn't want to forget her.'

Sam, a woman counsellor, was very surprised at the time grief took when she had a miscarriage of her first pregnancy: 'That was the thing that shocked me most, the amount of time it took me to grieve that loss. When I think of the subject of loss and bereavement, that's the one thing I feel strongly about. No matter how much time you allow yourself, it always takes more.'

Sam is now in her late thirties and has two children. At the time of the miscarriage she was a teacher. 'Even though I had a lot of support, did loads of crying and ranting, and expressed an awful lot of feelings about the loss, immediately I went back to work I found myself being tearful again. I had taken a couple of weeks off in any case, and I felt guilty about taking more time, but I had to. I was very shocked, having been given lots of time, that it still wasn't enough, and this is what has been important to know about grief. I've noticed it in other people since then: either they, or the people with them, expect the process to be much shorter than it is.'

She found it was important not to try to conceive again before she had properly mourned the loss of this first baby, and it was five months before she was able to consider another pregnancy. The wait was partly to feel she had resolved the mourning process, and could look forward to a new baby rather than back towards her lost one. It was also so that she would be strong enough – at least in theory – to cope if the same thing happened again. For in learning that miscarriage is not uncommon, she feared being one of the women who go through a number of pregnancies before having a live birth. Fortunately, her next two pregnancies resulted in healthy babies.

Time and loss have an intricate relationship. If looked at in a certain way, all of life involves loss because all of life involves spending or using up time. Time is life's gift, and from the moment of birth it is finite for everyone – and ticking away. Every minute 'gained' is also a minute which is 'lost'. This is the paradox of being alive. Time is finite in a human life and, like the book that was read by the woman whose first remembered grief was finishing it, days mount up on one side and run out on the other.

How the book is read or experienced, whether the pages or days on the left-hand side are still referred to and whether they are viewed as a dead story or a living one, depends on the reader. Or perhaps, more accurately, it depends on the reader's view of loss and gain. The left-hand side of the book can be seen as days lost, or as experience gained, as time irrevocably spent or as a store, a wealth of life lived and memories which can be called on for present and future use. In other words, yesterday is either accumulated time or dead time, depending on one's viewpoint.

In a culture which promotes life in the fast lane there is a tendency to rush through life itself, and certainly through grief, and to have little regard for yesterday. So it is easy, but dangerous, to view the past and grief as a waste of time, thereby laying in a vast store of trouble for the future. For grief which is not attended to, or which is unresolved, has a habit of reappearing in strange, persistent and painful ways. If loss is not resolved, it does not disappear, but waits its chance to assert itself and to cause trouble – with accumulated, compound interest – at a later date.

The ability of unresolved loss to trouble people years after a death or trauma was discussed by many people. Sue, who is now in her early forties, spoke of a similar experience to the woman who suffered unbearable facial pains when a relationship ended (see chapter 4). Sue described physical pain as being the spur to discovering what had lain hidden in herself for many years after the death of her mother. She was twenty-four when her mother died of breast cancer after battling with the illness for ten years. She had thus been ill since Sue was in her early teens. In the last six months of her life her family – a husband and two daughters – knew she was going into irreversible decline, so they all had time to prepare for her death. Nevertheless, some time after this, physical symptoms began to affect Sue, her younger daughter, and they persisted for about fifteen years: 'Within a couple of years of her death I started to have strange back and then stomach pains. Before that, it began with dizzy spells and diarrhoea, and I would be on the verge of passing out if I didn't eat when I needed to. There was very little time between feeling I needed to eat and feeling I was going to pass out.'

Extensive tests over a number of years failed to find anything wrong with Sue, except a slightly low blood sugar count, which she received treatment for. The physical pains, however, continued, and she was eventually referred to a psychotherapist. It was this work, still continuing, which brought her to the root of the pain she was feeling: 'We were a family who didn't talk. In the two or three years before my mother died I lost all my grandparents. That wasn't talked about either. Neither was my mother's illness. And yet she altered so much physically. They didn't have chemotherapy in those days, and she had radiotherapy. Her arm became huge. Then she started developing all this body hair. Then her face got fat and moon-like, and it was just disgusting what was happening to her. And I couldn't help. I couldn't do anything at all about it. I was trogging off to school every day, and we didn't talk about any of it. That was the problem.'

Sue was reluctant to talk about the grief outside her home: 'Not only did we not talk at home, but we didn't talk *at all*. One or two people at school must have asked me how she was, and I just said OK and didn't go into details.' While accepting now that this reticence was part of her shyness, she feels it was universal, citing an example of another girl at her school who did the same thing when her younger brother was killed: 'Her brother died in a road accident and it was shocking that someone even younger than yourself should be killed. From that day on she never mentioned his name once. It's as if he'd never existed. And her mother kept his room exactly as it was for years.'

During the course of therapy, which she has been in for two and a half years, Sue's back and stomach pains have diminished. She has no doubt that this has happened because at last she has taken the time and effort to unravel the trauma of her mother's ten years of illness, as well as her death: 'When I first started to see him [the therapist], my mother was so much on my mind. Even fifteen years later, I just talked and talked about my mother until I'd talked it all out.

'I was a late developer as a teenager, and he explained that I was coming into puberty as she was getting sick and a role reversal began to take place very much at the wrong time. I was supposed to try to take care of her at that point, and I didn't know how to because I felt so immature myself. I also felt completely impotent about her illness. There was nothing at all I could do to stop it.'

All of this was made worse because Sue seemed to rely upon her mother to a larger degree than most teenagers. Her shyness coupled with being a late developer meant that her mother's illness made her very frightened: 'She was my world, and as well as that, she was a buffer between me and the world outside, protecting me from it. The first time I saw her cry – I was about twenty at the time – I felt as if it finished me. I felt as if I was done for. It was Mother's Day and I gave her a card saying how wonderful she was and she burst into tears and said no, she wasn't, she was hopeless and ill. I was shocked, and I didn't know what to do.'

Because of the help she has now received, Sue can applaud her mother's tremendous courage and tenacity in living for ten years with an illness which was fatal. During that time she took her children out, and remained at home until the last four days of her life. Previously Sue's own hurt and loss, and the further hurt she suffered from not being able to deal with that loss properly, had masked her ability to celebrate her mother. She was unable therefore to draw strength from her, from the knowledge of her mother's courage and of her sense of purpose in staying alive for her family. For many years she had also been hiding her guilt that even when her mother was on her deathbed she was physically repelled by the reality of her dying: 'She went into hospital on the Wednesday and died on the Sunday. She had been fine when I first went in, but when I went in to see her on the Saturday, I thought I was going to be sick or pass out. My stomach was rising up into my throat. She was barely lucid, and I was shaking life a leaf. I was thinking, I mustn't throw up all over the bed. That would be awful. I had to leave.

'Did I say goodbye to her? No. Me saying goodbye would have been completely out of place with everything that went on in our family. But the whole scene is still there in my mind, complete, and it lives with me. I felt I behaved badly.'

The experience of physical pain was talked about often by people suffering grief. Usually it went away after a few weeks or months, so it can be thought of as part of the grieving process. Depending on one's viewpoint, it may be seen as severe stress or as a physical manifestation of an unresolved emotional grief. Both, in fact, are the same thing. The people who mentioned having this – or any other severe distress – and who took care of it straight afterwards did not then seem to suffer it later; it slowly went away. People who suffered distress and did not report remembering pain at the time seem to have had subsequent problems. In other words, if not attended to at the right time, the grief goes underground and then re-emerges.

'At the right time' is a phrase worth investigating, for part of time's role within grief is its demand for things to happen when appropriate. It cannot be held up in an effort to avoid grief – 'I'll get on with life now and grieve later' – without there being consequences. These were described by another woman who lost her mother six years ago when she was in her early thirties, an age when she was old enough to cope better. She believes she has still not resolved issues arising from the way she delayed grieving over her mother's death. They stem mainly from the fact that mourning was made difficult for her because she was not close to her mother, as her sister was, something which went back to when she was a small girl.

She recognised there was a problem in her life relating to the death of her mother when she found the fifth anniversary of the death painful: 'I found it very upsetting at a time when I thought I was over it. But I'm not in a way. My mother died, and within six months a long-term relationship with a man who was important to me also ended. I began to realise some things, like how much I keep people at a distance – and how much I kept my mother at a distance. I never confided things in her. I kept them to myself. Now that I don't have a mother I realise how nice it would have been to have done that, to have confided.

'My mother died of cancer of the spine, and the process of her dying was so painful for us all that I felt completely numb at the time. Death is so final. I was there when she died, and just seeing someone die is extraordinary. You see someone move from the state of being a person to being an inanimate object – and there's nothing you can do about it. Absolutely nothing.'

She thinks that she accomplished the grieving process badly, and that it held fears for her, like the fear of her own death from the same illness as her mother. But she also feels that her present knowledge of that will make a difference to her own future. By 'taking time out' to face up to some losses she had kept hidden from herself, she is now stronger and more optimistic: 'I tried to shelve the grieving process. I was tired of it, tired of crying. But it kept on seeping back. It does that. You think you've closed the door, and it seeps back under it. It hits you at the kitchen sink and when you're not expecting it. But there were things I hadn't faced. I hadn't faced my regret that I shall now never be able to say things to my mother I would have liked to.' What kind of things does she mean? She hesitates, and then says: 'I would like the opportunity of talking to my mother now about how I might have made her feel. It's a mistake I made, and I see other people doing it – it's as clear as the nose on your face. They are angry with their parents, and they don't deal with it at the right time, which is when it's happening. I was angry with my mother – who knows exactly why? – and I always kept her at arm's length. I must have made her feel useless, and I really regret that and would like to be able to talk about it, about why it happened and what she felt about it . . . '

The fact that unresolved grief can cause pain ten, twenty or forty years after a loss shows that time – by itself – does not necessarily heal anything. Rather, it allows layers to grow over problems which then either seep out or erupt later on. Time is certainly part of the healing process, but only if it is spent accepting, tending or being creative with an emotional wound rather than avoiding it. A GP who sees a considerable proportion of patients who are in grief says that she often explains the importance of expressing emotional pain by drawing analogies with physical illness: 'I first of all ask people in for a chat. I remember one woman phoned the surgery after the sudden death of her husband. She wanted to remove his name from our list of patients. We didn't know he'd died at the time because she'd phoned an ambulance and he'd been taken to hospital and died there. She was quite calm, and when I asked her to come in and see me she said: "Oh no, doctor, you've got better things to do. I don't want to waste your time, and it's not as if I'm ill." '

The GP persuaded her patient that if not exactly ill, she was certainly unwell, and that if she did not take some time now, she might need a good deal more at a later date. When the woman came in 'it was obvious she was still in shock, and I explained to her that grief was an emotional blow in the same way that being hit was a physical blow. She hadn't cried in the thirty-six hours since her husband's heart attack, and when I talked about how if you received a physical blow it hurt, and bruised you, and even caused broken bones that needed time to mend, she began to cry. She could understand it that way, and she could have some compassion for herself.'

The GP considers many of her patients are 'hard on themselves' with emotional traumas, taking the attitude that if you ignore something, it will go away. Many also take the view that time will heal everything and thereby cause themselves extra grief. 'I tell them bluntly that the only thing time can do by itself is tick by, and it's how you use it that matters. That's why I find the analogy with physical illness so helpful. I say that if they had a bad burn or a broken leg, they'd do more than carry on as before and let it sort itself out. "It needs a bit extra" is what I hear myself saying.'

The 'extra' is quite often just an acknowledgement that a deep wound has occurred and is important. It is also, perhaps, the ability or willingness to view time itself slightly differently: not only as a linear, one minute following the next progression, but as something that has depth as well as length.

Ellen, who lost a close childhood friend when they were both in their thirties, feels this happened to her – that she managed, eventually, to create out of her friend's death a way of experiencing time which has made her live a much fuller, richer life. Now in her forties, she says: 'I think I've learned more through her dying than I'd learned in all those years before. It's been a real eye-opener for me.' What has she learned exactly?

'I've learned that giving people time is more important than anything else. It sounds simple, but I hadn't done it before Anna died. I've always been a busy person. She was much calmer than me, and it took her dying to make something clear to me. To put that "something" in a nutshell, Time with a capital T is all there is in life, and that's what I learned; that I was using it – time – up at a giddy rate of knots, and – forgive the pun – like there was no tomorrow.'

Ellen had spent her life using time up, rushing through it, rather than 'having' or experiencing it: 'I'd got to the age of thirty-five without realising that there isn't anything else except time that we have to give each other anyway. But I hate clichés like "quality time", so I'll try to explain it in a different way.'

For Ellen, life, the fact or process of being alive, now seems quite different. It is as if time itself has taken on an important new dimension. Previously she was always conscious of the next thing she had to do, and always pushed for time. Now, while the physical duration of a minute or an hour is exactly the same, the experience of it is quite different: 'Before Anna died life *felt* like a race to me. I achieved a great deal, but inside it's as if I was permanently squeezed. Now I achieve just as much, in fact, more. I think the nearest I can get to describing it is that I don't bludgeon each minute of the day over the head like I used to. Instead I seem to experience what time feels like – and that gives me proper time to do everything I need to, and to enjoy being alive.'

There is no doubt that time has a completely different quality if experienced for what it is rather than something to be metered. The phrase 'take your time' expresses this. It suggests that time is ours to be taken hold of, or held, not charged through at top speed. Ellen, who was born in America but has lived in Britain for most of her adult life, stays in this country because 'things happen at a slower pace here'. Returning to her friend's death, she says: 'I now feel as if I'm experiencing my own life rather than charging through it. Anna's death has given me that. And when I think I'm moving too fast again, I think of her and slow right down. That way I have more time, not less.'

This has a paradoxical quality to it, reminiscent of some of the great religious truisms. In Taoism, for example, there is a saying about personal power that a truly wise, powerful person travels through life like an empty boat – *not* creating waves. And according to a Christian maxim, a person who tries to save her or his life will lose it while a person who gives it up will save it. So it seems with time. Someone who tries to make the most use of it by frantically filling it up may be losing out. Someone who is truly relaxed and who appears to waste time may be achieving far more in terms of knowing what it is like to be alive.

An American colleague believes we 'treat time like a bank account, a charge card. You take a bit out of that account and put it into the other. You spend a bit, save a bit, and by the time you drop dead you haven't had one minute you can seriously call your own. God's an accountant, for Heaven's sake! – with a stop-watch in his hand.'

One of the creative things grief does is to give us the chance to view time differently. For grief sometimes gives the impression of stopping time, and also of making it, or at least the pain experienced, seem endless. It renders time in the 'clock on the wall' sense relatively meaningless. It swipes ordinary hours or concepts of time sideways, by making them both stop and go on for ever. The life, the time, of a person one loves has stopped, and one single sleepless night after that can, initially, seem like an eternity. As with Terry, who said that death temporarily stopped the future, so grief puts time on hold as well as into a different perspective.

A woman in her mid-thirties described the problem with time that she experienced in two awful nights a few weeks after the death of her much loved father. When she left the hospice bedside where he died, he was still warm, still the father she loved. It was the shock of seeing him laid out, 'feeling like marble', in the crematorium days later which caused the bad nights when this 'marble figure' came to trouble her. 'I woke up in the middle of the night absolutely terrified. I thought someone in the room had coughed, and that there was someone there. This happened again the next night, and I lay there completely unable to move, even an inch. I just lay in absolute, complete, total terror.'

As the night ended and light came in the bedroom window, she had the first inkling of what this terror was, and why it was happening: 'As my body began to unfreeze, and I felt I could begin to move, I realised two things. The first was that I had been petrified to move one single inch in case I touched the marble figure of my father. I was afraid to turn round in bed in case this marble figure was lying next to me. No, not "in case", it was because I actually believed the figure was there. I believed it was my father who had coughed.

'The second thing I realised is where the "time" element comes into it. This nightmare was having such a devastating effect on me because I thought this might happen for the rest of my life, that it would never stop. My mind was whirring and it was saying, what about if this lasts for ever? What about if this is what happens after a death, and it never ends? If this never ends, I can't bear it, I shall go mad or commit suicide.

'You see, I loved my father. I respected him as a man and I loved him as a person. And I was horrified to feel afraid of him, and I was horrified, in those two nights, that I was going to spend the rest of my nights, the rest of my life, like that, waking up in fear of the father I loved.'

In the days following these awful nights she spoke with friends and sought out other people who had lost relatives, and she discovered that what she was afraid of was not her father, but the 'marble figure' in the mortuary. Yet she had wanted to see him there, to say her last goodbye, and is now pleased that she did. 'I realise that my father himself left me when he was still warm, and that the figure in the mortuary was not my father, but a dead body. My father had already gone. So I didn't need to be afraid of that body, for it wasn't my dad.'

One of the many potentially frightening aspects of loss in terms of its relationship to time is that it does not end for good. It continues, for although an important loss can be recovered from, what or who has been lost cannot be fully replaced, at least not with an identical substitute. But as a bereavement counsellor explained: 'Loss continues, ironically, for those who won't – or can't – face it. People who *do* face it recover, and they are able to find new relationships, new friends, new jobs and new hopes. The people who *don't* recover are the ones who bury the loss inside themselves, and it might take years, but it comes out one way or another.'

She gave the example of a mother who was thirty-four when her fifteen-year-old daughter got pregnant. The daughter wanted to end the pregnancy, but the mother was insistent she have the baby. When the baby was born, the mother than 'took it over completely' and the daughter began to be very resentful that, having been forced by her mother to give birth to a child, her mother then 'stole' him from her. The counsellor said: 'It turned out that the mother had had an abortion herself at sixteen, something she'd never forgiven herself for. When she got pregnant again – at eighteen – she kept the baby, even though she had no support from her family or the child's father.

'But she didn't stop feeling guilty about that first pregnancy and grieving for the loss of that first child. When her own daughter got pregnant, she saw it as a way of making up for what she'd done. She took great care of the child, and she couldn't see that she was taking over from her daughter. The daughter felt completely left out, and her feeling that her mother had "stolen" her baby was understandable. Her mother had. She had taken over her daughter's child to make up for the loss of her own . . .

'This was one of the few cases where a family tragedy ended up having a good outcome. Because they both came for counselling – initially due to the daughter's age – they came to an understanding of what had happened, and it was decided they would share the baby. This meant the daughter could return to school, which she wanted to do, but still have a big part to play in her baby's life.'

By not accepting her own loss at the time, this teenager's mother was unable fully to recover from it because she was not paying attention to what the loss required or demanded of her. A psychotherapist said that for recovery to occur, the person in grief needs to accept that a loss has happened, and to feel the consequences of it. If the consequences are felt at the time, they seem to begin to produce their own 'remedy'.

This varies from person to person: no two people seem to be alike in the way – and particularly the order – in which they experience the various emotions that can be involved in loss. With sleep, for instance, which is an essential part of any cure, some people will first of all sleep heavily, their remedy being rest from the pain. Others will barely sleep at all for a while, but as the psychotherapist made clear, that is their remedy: 'The received wisdom is that the stages of grief, such as anger, guilt, fear, withdrawal, denial, acceptance, get jumbled up in different people and happen at different times. So it's not possible to say, for example, that in general people will move from one stage to another in a set order. Neither is it possible to predict what people's needs will be. Grief is very individual. Some people will sleep, and then go through a period of wakefulness; others will get very little sleep. Some people will go through many cycles of sleep patterns, or anger or guilt before the grief is resolved or absorbed. Others will have relatively gentle griefs.

'Not only will the timing be different for different people, but also the amount of time.'

The wish to avoid spending time on grief, in the belief that it is 'wasted' or 'dead' time, leads people away from help rather than towards it. What it seems to do is to stop time or retard development at the point at which the unaccepted grief occurs. A counsellor described this: 'Certain older people do try to stop time anyway, by saying that they don't want to go on. They seem to be saying: "I will stay here, stuck like this, for ever." But it's the people who are young enough and flexible enough to change, and who won't, let's face it, accept being hurt, who cause the real problems. They really stop the clock.'

The paradox is that the person who is unwilling or unable to accept being hurt cannot be made better. All our hopes and wishes for them will not help if they have not, themselves, first allowed themselves to recognise their pain, for it is this pain which responds to our offers of kindness and is warmed by them. If the pain is not acknowledged, not all of our crying, dancing on our hands, turning somersaults will do. The person makes her or his own resistance our impotence – and the rest of the world's too – by stopping the clock at the point where a severe loss happens. She is Miss Haversham in *Great Expectations*; he becomes the Scrooge for all future Christmases.

A person who will not accept either being hurt or the grief arising from it stops time, and they then need to steal it back from the rest of us. As with the mother who needed to take over her daughter's baby, they even 'steal' across generations. Those of us who will not or cannot be healed also steal time in other ways, and become, in fact, various kinds of thieves, or time bandits. In the main we steal attention. We steal other people's time by being continually needy. We also steal vitality and hope away from the common pool which so badly needs such commodities. In other words, we are a drain. For if we fear bothering other people with our hurt and taking up their time, the irony is that we take up far more in the long term by not allowing ourselves to grieve.

That we view time as life's gift may explain why the thought of spending it on a seemingly negative activity like grieving goes so against the grain. There is a strong tendency to wish to 'get over grief' as quickly as possible in the belief that it is a backwater which we must swiftly steer out of. Grief so easily gives the impression of being a period of stagnation, but it is a time when deep, renewing forces are at work. These forces contain the potential power of our healing and of our ability to wish to continue with life. They contain time's seeds, if you like: the beginning of imagination, a feeling of sadness rather than emptiness, the first break in a grey horizon, a portent that it is seldom too late for 'life to go on'.

* * *

CHAPTER 9

Resurrections

How acknowledging grief is more rewarding than denying it

The opportunity to be creative following a loss or a grief was emphasised during interviews for this book. Echoing the words of Ellen in the last chapter, who talked of shaping time to her own life rather than her life to the clock, another woman, Lorna, revealed what she had learned in the years following the death of her sister. They were both in their twenties when her sister died, and Lorna, who is now in her early forties, was aware of an extra 'fullness' in her life after she had got over the grief: 'Life is sometimes very sweet because of the memory of her. She would have been forty next year and sometimes when I'm working in the garden or when I'm walking out in the hills I think how I would dearly love to know what kind of woman she would be now. What would my sister be like at forty?

'I find the memory of her is a kind of focus for what is good in my life – and hopeful. She had a wonderful spirit and when I think of her, it urges me on; it makes me do things, good things. She had a warm smile, and that smile of hers is behind things like wanting to reach the top of the next hill. I think I'm too tired to do it, and I turn to go back down again and then I smile too, and I push on. It's as if the fact that she's dead makes me more glad, more determined to be alive.'

As the death of her friend has deepened Ellen's perception or experience of time, so Lorna has found that the memory of her dead sister affects the intensity of her sight and hearing: 'I see things with extra eyes, and hear things in a keener way. I can't describe it any better than that. Standing on a mountain-top looking at the view, I sometimes turn to go – and then turn back again and look *properly*. I've seen it once, but I look again, and it's the second time that I take it in. It's the same with music. I listen, and then I stop and I say: "No, *really* listen." I've become used to it now. If I'm not looking or hearing properly, something inside me pulls at me, tugs at me. I feel I hear and see more fully because of my sister's death. It's up to me as the person who's living to see and hear as fully as I can. Does that make sense?'

In making creative sense of her sister's death, Lorna has managed to retain her sister's presence in her daily life, and to make her own life fuller, richer, because of it. This chance is missed by people who deny grief or loss, and wish no part of it. In denying this creative opportunity, others are denied as well. A journalist colleague, Daniel, when asked once what he felt 'happened' after people died, replied: 'The dead are held in trust in the hearts and minds of the living. It's up to the living what happens to the dead.' This implies that the living 'do' something about the dead. If they accept the pain of the loss, they create from the memory of the dead a fuller present and a richer future. If they deny the pain, this work cannot be carried out.

'Doing for the dead' is a service we imagine belongs only to churches, temples, mosques and gatherings of people in the name of religion, for a very obvious way in which religion comes into grief is through the burial or cremation of the dead. Religions also, of course, bring up, or resurrect, the question of time, since all mainstream religions concern themselves with resurrection through the concept of eternity or everlasting life. Everlasting life means that those of us who believe in it are offered time on a grand scale – that is, the prospect of eternity.

Religions are also, of course, inducements or encouragements to 'good' behaviour. The moral question of what is viewed as 'good behaviour' has been something religions have fought over and people have died for in their hundreds of millions. The idea of being offered 'remission for good behaviour' (the irreverent comment of a man in his mid-twenties) has not escaped a man in his late sixties who has remarried since the death of his first wife twenty years ago. Although not religious, he was brought up as a Christian, and gives an unusual slant on the potential problem created in his life should there turn out to be heavenly accommodation: 'My first wife was a wonderful, good person and I didn't stop loving her when I married my second wife. But I do love my second wife, who is also a good, kind person. I love them both as different people at different times. My question is this: If there was a heaven, which wife would I live with? It's a case for saying there is no heaven, otherwise what happens to people when someone dies and they remarry?'

For those who do not practise religion – the majority – heaven, nirvana or eternal life can seem to have been created to comfort us for the inevitability of death. They are on offer, as one woman put it, 'for the faint-hearted who would prefer not to face the fact that our time really is limited, and very precious because of that'.

Some people 'turn to religion' for a short while, or even for their lifetimes, following a death, as most of the clergy are aware. But for those who are not religious and do not continue to believe in an afterlife, who only accept it temporarily as a way of softening the blow of the disappearance of a loved one, what, I asked an Anglican vicar, does a church offer people in grief? He replied: 'Sometimes you can help them take better care of the living.' He believes most grief is caused not through deaths, but through poor relationships, and recounted what happened once when a family who had lost two children in tragic circumstances came to see him: 'We were discussing the funeral arrangements, and I was having a bit of difficulty working out who was who because a whole crowd of them came to see me. I knew who the parents were, but there was a man I couldn't quite place. The father was pale and drawn and said very little, but the mother was in floods of tears. We were working out hymns and an order of service when the mother suddenly turned to this unidentified man and in between sobs shouted at him: "You've got children. Why don't you talk to them? We've lost ours and you don't even talk to yours." She then completely broke down.

'It turned out the man was her brother, and he had a twenty-year-old son. The relationship was very bad between them. Effectively they weren't speaking. The man afterwards came to see me by himself, and I think I was able to help. He was able to tell me in confidence *why* he couldn't talk to his son.

'It often takes a death to bring people close, to break down everyday barriers and release pent-up emotions. Then, people feel, it's too late. But my message to religious or non-religious people is, it isn't too late. If there's one living person you can form a better relationship with because you're shocked or hurt by a death, then do it.'

The vicar said that a death in a family brings out both kindness and anger, and that it acts as an important release for emotions which often have long histories. He sees a death in a family therefore not only as a loss, but as the possibility for change. In other words, someone's death can bring life to a surviving relationship.

He has what would be called a liberal interpretation of the Christian Gospels: 'My understanding of the Resurrection is that it is in the gift of all of us to be resurrected through the death of someone close to us. We can do it every day of our lives. It simply means that we honour the living, beginning with ourselves, and that we take the opportunity afresh to love while we can. That's what resurrection is – new, daily love. It's not death that's the problem, you know. It's knowing how to live.'

Knowing how to live is an essential part of knowing how to cope with the pain of grief, and of learning in a creative rather than a destructive way how to resolve it. So many people spoke of there being two clear ways to go after a severe loss: 'life or annihilation'; 'living in the past or looking to the future'; 'looking to the living or to the dead'; and 'being bitter or getting on with life'. Most had chosen the latter option, getting on with life, and a few mentioned 'resurrection'.

The word 'redemption' was used by the woman quoted in the previous chapter who was frightened of the 'marble figure' of her father. She is a regular churchgoer, and believes that her father lives on in another life. This does not lessen her present pain in losing him, but she feels that the pain has already brought her mother and herself, and certain members of her extended family, even closer: 'We have said some truly lovely things to each other, some wonderful things, things you don't normally say, about love and about how much we mean to each other. It took my father dying for one of my uncles to tell me that my dad had always been his hero, and that he'd always looked up to him as a fine, good man.

'I think grief does that to you. It's a very powerful emotion. It's already made me fear for my sanity and cry in my mother's arms like I haven't done since I was a small child. I think the best word for it is "redemption". My dad's gone. We can't do anything about that, but we can redeem what's left, which is to go to the living for comfort, and to tell them that we love them.'

The ability of deaths to change, to redeem or to resurrect the living was talked about by a man in his fifties who lost his wife and child in a car crash: 'It lays you completely low. Knocks you out, and, looking back on it, I was ill, debilitated for months, maybe years. And all the time you're thinking, I must get back to strength, I must fight this. Then one morning you wake up and see some sense to it all. Not sense to them dying – who knows about that? I certainly don't – but sense to how to *live* with them dying. That's the trick. You can't do anything about life's accidents, but you can help what you do about them after they've happened.'

What had he done?

'For a start I don't have any truck with trivialities like worrying about if I'm ten minutes late for a meeting . . . ' He hesitated and then continued: 'The best way I can explain it is that deaths either wake you up or put you to sleep; they make you better at living, or they take you with them. Forgive me being blunt about this, but there's only two ways to go. And most of us have the choice. Not all, but most.

'And if you get better at living, then life becomes quite precious. Small things, like smelling the air on a clear day. That's the religious flavour to it, the resurrection. I'm not religious myself and I don't believe in an afterlife. To me death is a mystery, and I'd prefer it to stay that way, unknown and unknowable to the living. But I do believe in life *now*. That's the secret. Living.'

He concluded: 'There are only two ways to respond to a personal tragedy. You stay in it for ever, and you punish yourself and everyone around you for what you've suffered.

You either choose the path of *deathliness* and *punish* life for what it's done to you, for your hurt and your loss, or you go for the second option and you live more fully and, yes, more lovingly.'

This wish to make sense out of death and to build a new or richer life happens when the lives of those who have died can be celebrated. And also where the death happens through no fault of those left behind. The problem is when a person is 'lost' to us through divorce, desertion or, as with the man who wished he had not found his father, disaffection or neglect. There are, similarly, difficulties when we had a poor relationship with the person who has died. It would seem hard to create from a poor relationship the opportunity for the kind of extra depth to life and the resurrection people have spoken of.

This in itself helps to explain something about loss or grief which seems puzzling at first sight: why it is generally the case that people who have lost good relationships fare better than people who have lost bad ones. In other words, why it is that people who have lost 'most' should regain strength, while people who have, seemingly, lost 'least' often do not. The man just quoted and Lorna, the woman whose feelings about the loss of her sister were described at the beginning of this chapter, both give implicit explanations of why this should be the case. The answer lies with love.

It seems that love, or the capacity to love, does not die, but on the contrary finds its own way of regenerating itself. Where there is no love, however, there is little to create with, and a tendency then to invent or reinvent the past, as discussed in chapter 7. A bereavement counsellor explained the creative presence of love: 'If the relationship has been good, the "love element" in it rescues the remaining person from their grief. The ability to love doesn't go away, even after someone has died. And you'll find these people usually find other good relationships. They often remarry.

'It's when people don't have the ability to love, where their relationships have been "disappointing" or even abusive, that you get the real problems. They're angry the person has gone – and they often stay that way. They become bitter and they don't trust people when, really, it's themselves they don't trust.

You can get over being hurt. You can get better. Especially if it's not your fault. People who had bad relationships carry on hurting because part of the bad relationship *was* their fault – and they only stop if you can help them to see that – and forgive *themselves*.'

The counsellor sees a number of people for whom anger is a predominant and continuing emotion in grief; many of them are suffering not so much grief as rage: 'Anger is a part of any grief, but where it seems to be the *only* part, you get the feeling that the person is not so much grieving a lost person as grieving a lost self. They can't cope by themselves, and they take all that out on the dead person. If they loved the person who died, they would be able, quite soon, to forgive them for dying, and they wouldn't keep on being angry.'

To forgive a person for dying might at first seem a strange concept, but it is an opportunity presented by grief, whether or not the person who died, or left, was loved. Terry, who felt insulted by the inappropriate use of the cliché 'time will heal', also had a sense of having to forgive his wife – for leaving him: 'Although she had been ill for a number of months and we'd had time to say our goodbyes, and to talk about the things we needed to, after she'd gone I still had this amazingly powerful feeling that she didn't love me. I've talked with other people since who have lost someone they love, and they say the same thing. With me it went on for several weeks, the feeling that if she'd loved me enough, she wouldn't have died. It's strange, I know.'

The act of forgiveness, of forgiving the dead for leaving us when we would dearly have loved them to stay, is an important aspect of grieving for a person who has died. For people who have deep or protracted griefs it is part of the process of re-emerging into the world as a person who is ready to trust again. It is also one of the differences – at least initially – between grieving for a dead person and a departed, living one. For it would be unrealistic in the early stages of abandonment to forgive a person for walking out on you. Being able to do that eventually, however, is an important element of knowing that the hurt has been recovered from.

In the case of a bad relationship where the person has died, it might seem as if the opportunity for forgiveness has passed, but only if the dead are viewed as having no inner life in the hearts and minds of the living. If they are, as Daniel the journalist remarked, 'held in trust', the living can bring about change. This was expressed by a man in his late forties called Paul, who has two children of his own and was in the process of writing something about his 'difficult' father when he heard of his death. The writing was a story, not a diary, and presented in the third person. In the early part of the story a man (Paul himself) is at a family funeral, that of an uncle, and he is standing with his father:

> Men were mostly absent in his family, as far as he could work out . . . being insignificant, doing nothing worth the telling. The women were the business.
>
> Except for his own father, of course. Life's natural bastard. He had always been around, most of all when you'd wished he wasn't . . .

We are told of some of the old man's excesses as he walks with his son round the graveyard:

> 'Just look at them,' the old man snorted, pointing at a row of gravestones . . . He leant closer, peering through his spectacles. ' "To Our Dear Departed Mother, Always in Our Thoughts." Ha! Forgotten long ago, I bet. As soon as they got hold of the will. And this one – "Darling Davey. Not Dead, But Sleeping." Sleeping! Who are they kidding? If they believe that, if they think he's sleeping, why stuff him in a coffin and stick him into the ground . . . ?'

In the course of the story the father continues his sneering comments and goads his adult son into being insulting himself. For the son realises – at last! – that this is what the old man wants. It is all he can accept in the way of attention – insults. So when the father asks:

> 'And when I'm dead, what'll you write on my grave?' the son does not hesitate in replying:
>
> 'Good riddance, you old bastard.'
>
> And for the first time that day the old man is happy.

The story is only three pages long, and it has a two-line addendum:

> Eighteen months later, after a summer that never happened, the son touched his father's coffin and told him he loved him.

Paul considers his own children provide the new eyes through which old relationships can be seen and described afresh. His children were fond of their bad-tempered grandfather, as he was of them. Paul is glad his father lived so long: 'I think the relationship between grandparents and grandchildren is the key to what might have been between parents and children.'

In a sense the dead are resurrected by living people who are prepared to be their guardians, their keepers. They are 'kept alive' in people's thoughts and memories. A woman in her late eighties talks of how so many people she knew have now died: 'Grief has to have a spiritual dimension as you get older, otherwise you're done for, really. All the people who knew you when you were young have gone, but the memory of what you did together is very important.' She feels that retaining the dead in memory is a very important thing to do, as is continuing to relate to the living, particularly to grandchildren: 'Your children and grandchildren anchor you in the present, but the past is also important. Just because people are in the past, it doesn't mean they didn't happen, you know. How can I put it? The things I did with my own parents, with my husband, I *did* do. I didn't imagine them, any more than I imagined having my children, or they having theirs. Do you see what I'm getting at? Remembering the dead is an important part of living.'

This woman is not religious, and has the following to say about the idea of eternal life: 'I wonder if people invented heaven as a way of getting out of their responsibilities. Instead of remembering the dead themselves, they could rely on heaven to take care of them. I can't believe in people walking around up there. Which is fortunate, as it happens, because I can't believe in hell either. My mother used to say it was meant to frighten people into good behaviour, and it doesn't do anything of the sort.'

She issues a warning of a kind, however: 'At my age you can find your relationships are more with the dead than the living. If you're not careful, you can become cocooned, carrying all these memories, these inner voices, around with you. You have to allow them their "lives", these inner people, but you also have to be practical. You have to allow real voices, your grandchildren's voices, to pierce this cocoon, otherwise I think you're in danger of getting the balance wrong.'

Within this balance – this remembrance of people past and present – the grief for anyone's leaving is an essential part of their eventual 'staying' as influential forces who add to our repertoire and our ability to live fuller, richer lives. Within these fuller lives we do things we would not have done had we not suffered loss.

The woman mentioned in the last chapter who wished she had talked with the mother she kept at arm's length has, for example, tried to stop other people doing the same. She is quite forthright with people who have 'parent problems': 'When people talk to me about problems with their parents, I say they should deal with them while their parents are still alive. I get quite angry sometimes if people complain, and I tell them they should do something about it now, while their parents are still here, because they're just storing up trouble for themselves if they don't.'

Shirley, the mother who lost her only son in a sailing accident off the coast of Bermuda (see chapter 2), feels that ten years after his death she has had, nevertheless, one of the best years of her life. Shirley too finds life very precious, and for her there were only two ways to go after a loss of this kind – life or death. She thinks 'it changes you for ever. It's such an annihilating experience – but it's also a growing one. Basically when it happens to you, it's either life or annihilation. You have to decide.' A few months after her son's death she went to see the family doctor who had written them 'a wonderful letter': 'He'd known my son since he was a baby and he said what a happy family we were. And it wasn't until then that I realised he'd also lost a child. It was for medical reasons, which must have been very hard for him as a doctor. He said he was glad she'd gone because she would have been a cabbage if she'd remained alive.

And he told me: "You know, you can deal with this two ways. You can sit down and bemoan your fate and say: 'Why me?' Or you can get on and make the best of life." '

Shirley decided to 'get on'. She wrote about her son's death, and through an article which appeared in a newspaper received scores of letters from other people who had also lost children. The letters that particularly moved her were from people who had not lost children but who wanted to write to say they nevertheless shared her grief with her. One of these letters simply said: 'I too have a son called Ben and he's adventurous, and I share the loss of your son with you.'

Although she feels it took her many years to get over her son's death, they had had a good relationship, and it is that which has helped. 'There may be another phase of grief as one gets older, I don't know [she is in now in her early sixties], but in a curious way I've probably been happier in the last few years of my life since I actually came to terms with Ben's death than possibly I've ever been before.'

She thinks it is almost impossible to account fully for this, but during the course of grieving she came to accept something keenly: 'I was very aware of the fact that he was dead and I was alive. So if I was alive and he wasn't, I needed to really use that life. I needed to enjoy it because it was a gift. I have felt it ever since, that life is a very precious gift. And, if you like, it's extra precious because I was living for two.

'I wished at the time there had been a choice in the matter. It should have been me who had gone. That is the natural order of things. But you don't get a choice, and I could see him standing there cross-faced and saying: "Oh, Mum, for God's sake, there's nothing you can do about it. Get on with the next thing." I knew he'd be incredibly irritated with me if I was going around being a wet weekend in Wigan.

'Some experiences are life-giving and some are life-denying. If you've actually been to the bottom, and it is the most terrible thing that can happen to you, you can find life after that becomes important. I think I have a quality of celebration about me sometimes. It wasn't easily won, but, if you like, it's a better memorial to my son than if I was to go round with a long face.'

Whether or not it is feasible to do this – to live more lovingly – and how soon after a severe loss this is possible depends to a large extent on the nature of the lost relationship: people who have lost good relationships fare better than those who have lost bad ones; they already know how to love, and therefore how to forgive, and how to behave in a kind, forgiving manner both towards the memory of the person who has died – and towards themselves.

A number of people who had lost good relationships therefore found in the years that followed that although it still made them tearful, it also enriched them. For Marjorie, a woman in her early forties, joy was one of the emotions which eventually crept into the process of grieving the death of her father, which had taken place two years previously. They were close and had what she called 'a really nice relationship'. 'At times I'm still very sad about my father, but at other times I also have this sense of great peacefulness about him.' She thinks this is because in the year before her father died she went to Crete on holiday with her parents, and also to France. She realised that year that they were both getting older and, while it was not easy with a high-powered job, she made the time to spend with them. 'I have absolutely no sense of regret at all. The last time I saw my father was at the docks at St Malo when he came to wave me off on the ferry after a long weekend in Brittany. So I'm lucky, if you like. There was nothing that I wished I'd done differently, so I don't have that sense of self-castigation or regret that I recognise is very strong in other people.'

Like the woman who tells friends to sort out relationships with their parents now, Marjorie also takes friends to task: 'I have a male friend who doesn't see a lot of his father. The relationship between them is quite difficult. And I said to him I was so glad that I saw my father, and that things were all right between us. I told him: "I think you should get your relationship with your father on a better footing now while you've got the chance." '

She said that this friend had now been to see his father, and that one of the important things you learned from grief is to sort out things with the living. She also said something about the nature of grief which was, again, surprising at first: she did not want it to end, at least not completely. This was because the relationship with her father had been a good one, and therefore she felt it was right that she should always miss him, at least a little.

Marjorie explained she had been allowed to realise this through people helping her grieve fully, mainly by letting her know it was normal to feel absolutely awful for a while. 'Some people were very kind and let me talk as much as I wanted to. A particular colleague at work who had also lost someone said: "Yes, I felt like that too, and it is awful, and you will go on grieving for the rest of your life in some way, but it gets better."

'That was the message – not, don't worry, it will go away, but talk about it and it will get better. I did this. I talked, and I realised after a while I didn't want it to go away. I don't want ever to get to the point where I don't miss him. I don't want ever to stop missing him because if I did, he wouldn't have been important. And he was.'

She feels she owed her father a great deal of gratitude for the warm relationship they had had, and for the security it had given her: 'Although not an emotional man, he'd never left me in any doubt at all that he loved me dearly and was proud of what I did . . . But he was proud of me as a person . . . I think that was the best thing. It wasn't that I got a first and a Ph.D. and all this. He actually thought I was all right as a person. And from my point of view, I felt the same about him. Added to which, he was my father, and I loved him.'

One of the aspects of grieving that is so crucial to recovery is to feel that the grief has been experienced properly – and in one's own way. In other words, while the nature of grief has many general characteristics, its expression is individual. Marjorie, for example, found that she had a need to tell people her father had died, even people she did not know well. At certain meetings where she came across people perhaps only once or twice a year, instead of saying she was fine when they asked how she was, she said: 'Actually, I'm not too well because my father died recently . . . ' Yet she is usually quite a publicly reserved person.

For another woman, Aysha, who is now in her late forties, it was an evening at the cinema which opened the door between the suffocating inner world of her private grief and the rest of life. Her husband had left her and her withdrawal from the world in order to tend some of her grief in private had gone on too long. It was threatening her journey back out again. Aysha seemed very 'enclosed' or cut off from the world by her grief. This changed one night: 'I remember walking down the street to go and see a film with a man who had been a friend for many years, and it was awful. He was walking next to me, but I couldn't *feel* his presence or support. I almost wanted to cry out: "Help me, help me", and I think I didn't do that because I was afraid it wouldn't work.

'The film was Shakespeare, and I thought it would be difficult, in my state, to keep pace with it. Then a kind of transformation, or melting, happened. I became completely absorbed in the film. I lost myself in it, and whatever was cutting me off from the world just disappeared. I could hear, I could feel and I could connect.'

Aysha's feeling of alienation did not completely vanish, 'as if by magic': 'It wasn't as if I was suddenly "cured" of my grief. Life isn't like that, but my hope had returned. If my feeling of being cut off could vanish once, it could vanish again. That film was my first experience of being "normal" again, and it gave me the strength and the determination to return to the normal world.'

A return to the normal world, a sense of recovery, came about through Aysha losing her self, and therefore her grief, in a film. As the objects of desire discussed in chapter 3 are, for a while, ambassadors of the dead, so nature, art, talking, are facilitators for the living.

One woman's 'facilitator' related to the figure of Christ. Her son was killed in a car crash in his late twenties, and she had become divorced only a few months before the accident: 'I didn't imagine I would ever get over it, except that's not the right way of putting it I've now found out. You don't "get over" grief, as far as I'm concerned. You learn first of all to accept it, and then to live with it.'

She described what the experience had done for her in a spiritual sense: 'I've never been religious, although I've thought a lot about life's "big issues", and I think grief either turns you towards or against religion. With me it did something strange. I started thinking about the Crucifixion, or about Christ, probably because I was in so much pain myself. It's never really made sense to me, the way the story's been told. I've never been able to imagine someone I never met "dying for my sins". I could imagine being responsible for my own "sins", and that's what suddenly made sense.

'I felt that what was meant by the whole business of the Crucifixion in symbolic terms is that you have to learn to accept and be responsible for your own pain. The story goes that Christ did that, and I think that story means we all have to do it, and then there would be no need for someone else to have to do it for us. We all have to bear our own pain, and if we do that, we won't put pain out into the world for others to have to deal with.

'Basically I don't see why anyone else should be crucified for me. I reject that idea. But grief does hurt you, and you feel like a child again. You want to cry, and you want somebody to make you better. You even want the world to stop and attend to your wounds. For me, that's what the story of the Crucifixion means. You have to come to terms with your pain and heal yourself. Then you become a responsible adult.'

A man in his forties whose close friend died when they were both in their twenties and whose long-standing relationship recently ended made an almost identical comment about grief having the potential for making people adult: 'If you've never been hurt, then you're not a grown-up. Being hurt makes you learn about your resources, and it teaches you how to use and value them. People who don't get hurt, or *pretend* they don't get hurt, don't know themselves.'

Our response to the question of whether we allow a dead person to live on, whether we permit that non-religious 'resurrection', determines how we grieve – and how we view life, and death. The way we view death is especially important for how creative we are with our lives. If death is viewed as a stone wall, as a 'dead ending', or if it is viewed as something to be banished from our thoughts so that we live life as if death does not exist, we really miss the point.

For death is essential to life as we know it. It gives our lives a shape and a context. It also gives them urgency through its messenger, time. If there were no physical death, if people, like Humpty-Dumpty, could be put back together again, then, arguably, life would be pointless. Moral outrages like war or murder would have no significance because if you abolished death, no one could be killed or murdered. Time would also be meaningless, for it would have no end.

By being creative with the memory of the dead people within us, with our grief, by allowing them – and ourselves – resurrections, we do not so much defy death as work with it. There is no doubt that we grow in stature as a result.

Many people spoke of distinct qualities they had gained through allowing themselves to experience loss, and also qualities which they recognised in others. A woman in her late forties, Yvonne, recounted what happened to a friend's girlfriend after her friend had died. Yvonne was not very close to the girlfriend, who was in her late twenties: 'She was nice enough, but we had nothing to say to each other. She enjoyed dancing and drinking and having a good time, all the things I enjoyed myself when I was her age.' When Yvonne's friend died, however, this changed. 'It's an awful thing to say in such tragic circumstances, but it's as if she blossomed. She really grew up, and I discovered things in her I never thought existed, and I could almost say *didn't* exist before.'

Yvonne explained how she came to say something which has stuck in her mind every since, after a night when her husband and herself invited their friend's girlfriend round to dinner about three months after their friend had died: 'We'd had a lovely, warm time, and I felt she was really one of the family, someone we appreciated and cared for in her own right. I turned to my husband after she'd gone and said: "You know what's happened, don't you? The dolly bird's grown up."'

The ability to 'grow up' through grief, and to discover attributes in oneself or in other people, is something people who have suffered loss have said they value highly. Grief offers us the opportunity to become more adult, more responsible, more loving and more alive. It does this at a very high cost, but the alternative to 'paying up' – denial – exacts an even higher toll.

The vicar mentioned earlier in this chapter said that people who will not pay or who are frightened of paying the emotional cost which grief exacts end up far poorer. Continuing his theme of resurrection for the living through the opportunity for 'new, daily love', he said: 'At least the dead can't help being dead. The living can, and the living become lifeless and depleted and deathlike when they avoid understanding and sharing their griefs.'

He spoke of how forgiving the dead their trespasses is sometimes easier than forgiving the living theirs, especially when it comes to forgiving ourselves: 'In the very first instance we have to have compassion for ourselves. Whatever we have done, that is where forgiveness begins. So many of us, when we are hurt, secretly believe we have deserved this. We think this is our punishment that this person we love or relied on has been "taken from us". I don't believe that, and I don't believe my God, or anyone else's, punishes in that way. What I do believe is that we have to face our losses, not run away from them; we have to grieve, and then we live more fully.

'You hear it said of certain people "they'll be late for their own funerals". Well, far, far too many are early.'

* * *

CHAPTER 10

Mollifying the Vicar

Unexpected behaviour within grief

A number of unexpected feelings and attitudes that arise out of loss and grief are little talked about, mainly because people feel either guilty or embarrassed about them. There is, for example, a strong urge in some people to make grief competitive or comparative as a way of placing their own griefs in the centre of the stage and marginalising other people's. A woman called Noleen described an incident at a social event when this happened.

She had lost a child and been through a divorce fairly close together and was talking not about this, but about the plight of some children in a news flash on television that day. The woman she was speaking with turned to her and said: 'What do you know? You've never suffered. You don't know anything about it.' When Noleen explained that she had, in fact, suffered, which is why she felt so keenly for these children, the other woman was 'unimpressed'. Noleen gathered 'she had lost a husband a long time ago, and had obviously never recovered. But she isn't the first person I've met who seems to want to make a competition out of grief. There are people who don't believe you have been hurt unless you go around with a great, long face all the time.

'I think it's a very damaging attitude to want to score points out of tragedies. It's as if some people spend their whole lifetimes reliving their griefs as if nothing else has ever happened to them – or to anyone else. The grief is all they've got, and they use it, sometimes in quite offensive ways.'

Using grief like a weapon to keep one's own grief centre-stage and fend off any knowledge of other people's is, perhaps, understandable for a short time. Another mother, who had also lost a child, felt guilty in 'owning up' to the fact that for a number of months following her child's death she was consoled by the sight of an ambulance: 'I know it sounds strange – and horrible – because obviously an ambulance is somebody's pain. But it used to make me terribly happy when I saw one because I used to think, oh, it's not C. [her child]. And it can't possibly be him, and nobody can ever hurt him again. When the Falklands happened, I felt something similar: at least he can't be sent there. At least he can't be killed.

'I know it's dreadful to say that, that I was pleased, for a while, when I heard an ambulance. But it's the truth. It was one of the ways I got better, one of the tricks I used to help myself for a while.'

The truth about grief was something which the people I interviewed wanted very much to speak about, to try to save others from having to experience what they themselves had. They wanted to talk about the guilt they felt at the bad behaviour which sometimes accompanies grief, like being pleased to see an ambulance or, as in the case of a man who was in his forties when his father died, 'slipping off for some consolation through sex': 'I just felt this overpowering need during the week of my father's funeral when the whole family – my mother, sisters, aunts, uncles – were gathered in the house to go round to my girlfriend's . I sort of felt guilty about it, a bit like playing truant, but it didn't stop me doing it because it was a way of asserting or reaffirming life.'

Other people spoke about their embarrassment over the amount of noise their grieving made in the initial days and nights of loss. They all, both women and men, used animal terms to describe it. A man who had lost his wife said: 'My sister stayed with me for a week, and I'd get up in the night and just walk and howl. It must have been like a dog howling. I had to do it to try to blot out the pain. The pain was so severe it was almost immobilising, and it was a way of trying to ease it.'

One woman in her early seventies 'bayed like an animal' in the nights following the death of her husband, and another in her late thirties got a friend to take her out in the nights following her lover's death: 'We travelled out into the woods where I could make as much noise as I wanted. It was my only consolation. I crawled through the days, and at night I did this howling and wailing among the trees.'

People wanted to talk about the 'reality' of grief, its quirks as well as its pains, both in what they themselves felt and also in what they experienced from other people. They found that, in the main, grief was dealt with in two ways: either in hushed, reverential tones or as something to get over as quickly as possible. It was 'in the hands of the religious brigade', as one person put it, or the 'denial' camp, who wished you would 'return to normal'. The latter caused a woman in her seventies to say: 'It made me feel like a television set: "Normal service will be resumed as soon as possible."' The first six months following the death of her husband were among the most difficult of her life, not only because of the grief itself, but because of other people's attitudes to it: 'One of the worst things that happened was a visit from a man from the church. It wasn't the vicar, but some man who visited people. He got down on his knees in my living room and started praying and, honestly, I felt accosted. He barely knew me, and there he was kneeling against the settee with his eyes closed, spouting all this stuff about dear, departed souls, and I wanted to scream.'

While many people were helped by religious services, and by the people who conducted them, a number were also angry and alienated by the 'hushed, reverential tones' that grief is so often shrouded in. A man in his mid-twenties, when asked about people's attitudes following the premature death of his father, said: 'The thing that most pissed me off was the "wringing-hands" brigade. I felt lots of things after Dad died: guilt because I was away at the time, anger because he was too young to die, puzzlement about why he'd collapsed when he was so healthy, regret that I hadn't said goodbye to him. I was very confused, and I found out quickly that a lot of people who were asking you how you were wanted something for themselves, not you. It's almost as if *you* had to make *them* better.'

Even among his own circle of friends, there were people who thought he should be crying all the time – with them – and felt rather annoyed that he was not: 'They were trying to get me to tell them things, and saying: "You mustn't bottle it up." But I don't think I ever bottled it up. People tend to think that if you don't sit down and tell them straight away about it all, or you don't break down on their shoulder, then you're keeping it all in.' He learned, after a while, to tell people what they wanted to hear. What he himself wanted was sincerity and a kind of simplicity: 'What was good was people doing things, not so much going out of their way, but doing things because they really wanted to do them. It's like I didn't want people to do me favours because my father had died.

'The thing that really impressed me was when one of my friends just rang and said he'd like to come up for the weekend, and spend some time with me. Another said he'd booked a cottage in Wales and asked me to come and do some surfing with him. That was really good. I wanted people to do normal things, because they were my friends and because *they* wanted to do them, not because they were the right things to do.'

Trying to do the right thing for someone who has suffered a loss can have an aura of contrivance, or insincerity, to it. The motive is usually a wish to be kind, and the result is often awkwardness. Some people in their twenties felt put upon by other people's attitudes, rather than helped. Gareth, whose mother died five years ago when he was twenty, said: 'It was the religious comments that really made me angry. I don't object to people being religious, but they shouldn't force their views on you. Some people said things like 'she's with God now' and it doesn't help you if you don't believe in all that stuff. It makes you feel a lot worse. There were a number of times that happened, and it made me angry. It was imposing on me.'

What inappropriately reverential tones do is deny the complexity and the fullness of the needs which attend loss. They deny the 'hard' emotions involved. Something else they do not take into account is humour. Marjorie, who did not want to stop 'missing' her father, said that 'graveyard humour' was present in her close family within a few days of her father being cremated. She and her brother had decided to take their mother to Switzerland the following summer to scatter the ashes. When these arrived eight days after the funeral, they were heavier than she had imagined, and she was concerned about how to get them out of the country. Was a permit of some kind needed? Would they have to clear it with customs? 'Suddenly we all just roared with laughter because one of us said that if we tried to conceal them, we'd probably get had up for cocaine smuggling.'

Even on the day following her father's funeral they were all laughing, in between tears, about warm and amusing memories of her father. When the three of them went to Switzerland, carrying the ashes in a plastic bag, there was another incident which made them all laugh: 'We scattered some high over the Alps and then decided to scatter the rest on a favourite walk of Mum and Dad's by a lake. And again it was the graveyard humour coming out, which I know might shock some people. But we all took a handful and started scattering these ashes, and because they were in a plastic bag, the swans started coming over thinking we were going to feed them. We were feeling a bit tearful about this, but we also laughed at the same time. So that was all right. The whole thing about scattering the ashes was fine, and I felt a real sense of completion after that which I couldn't get at the time of the funeral [seven months earlier] because at that time I hadn't done enough grieving.'

Another woman, Frances, spoke about humour in relation to her father's funeral, this time connected to a mistake over parish boundaries. She, her two sisters and her mother had arranged the funeral, which took place in a rural part of northern England. They chose to bury her father in a small country churchyard near the family home without realising that it was a few hundred yards outside the parish boundaries, and their 'usual' vicar's domain. When a priest other than the vicar who had visited her father conducted the service, they thought it was because the vicar was on holiday or ill. However, he appeared at the wake, as Frances recalls: 'There we were, all back at the house at the wake, when the vicar turned up to visit my sick father, and we had to tell him he was dead. I know it doesn't sound at all funny – and isn't – but at the time we all just collapsed with laughter, my mother included. I think it was because the vicar was so angry we felt like naughty schoolgirls. We had all thought the vicar was on holiday. The vicar thought my father was still alive. Meanwhile my father was buried in the wrong parish. So, at my father's funeral, my mother had to spend half an hour mollifying the vicar.'

An undertaker explained why, particularly in his profession, humour is a part of the business: 'When you're working with people in grief you've got to give it your all, and you can't afford to make a mistake. It's always playing on your mind that you've got to get it right because the people who've employed you expect that, and you don't get a second chance.' The tension from always being on the alert for the slightest thing going wrong, as well as maintaining a calm exterior at the same time, meant that when work was finished, he and his colleagues had to find a way to relax: 'The way we unwind in this business is to play practical jokes on each other. Silly things, like throwing sponges at each other. Or someone will go to their limousine and find the seats have been screwed all the way forward.'

The other unexpected emotion that is seldom spoken of in relation to grief is sex, as one man in his late forties knows: 'There you've got the two biggest taboos, sex and death. You just try putting those two together.' Following the death of his wife, after more than twenty-five years of marriage, it was intimacy, rather than sex, he first of all craved: 'One of the physical things is that you're sleeping side by side with somebody for all those years. You don't have to be sexually active, but for all that time you've had a woman's body next to you. Then it's gone, and you want it back.'

A month or so after his wife died he found he wanted sex itself: 'I was greatly torn by wanting to go down and get a video or a sex magazine, and I didn't do it because I thought it would be disloyal. For about three months I resisted it, and then, just by chance, I slept with someone . . . ' This relationship did not continue because he was still guilty about having sex with another woman so soon after the death of his wife.

Another man, Douglas, also in his late forties, had a different experience, partly because he had only been involved with the woman he lived with for three years before she died. He did not feel guilty about having formed another sexual relationship within months of her dying because she had urged him to do that before she died: 'She wanted me to get on with my life, and to find someone else. She told me that I wasn't to grieve for too long because we'd already done a lot of our grieving together during the months that she was dying. She released me in a way.

'During our last year together, after she had got ill, I think I can literally count on the fingers of one hand the times we made love in that year, and still have fingers left over. Penetrative sex was painful for her. And although we were able to masturbate mutually and have an enjoyable experience together, I know she felt guilty about not having penetrative sex. There were a few occasions when she said: "Look, we can make love if you want to." And I said: "No. That's wrong, not because *I* want to. It had to be because *we* want to."'

Jenny, who is in her early thirties, lost her partner ten years ago after a relationship of which she says: 'It had never once crossed my mind what it would be like if we were not together.' She too found that sex played a significant role in the grieving process: 'I missed that part of the relationship very much, not only the sexuality, but the physical closeness. I couldn't stand sleeping on my own. That was one of the most distressing things, one of the things I missed most, his presence in bed. I really found it disturbing being alone at night.'

Jenny was nevertheless surprised to find that within days of her partner's death she began to masturbate: 'It happened so soon. But your body doesn't stop. That part of your life does not stop. Retrospectively I was terribly grateful that *as it happened* G. and I had made love the night before he died. Having been together for a while, we didn't always make love, but we had the previous night, and I was very glad of that. I'd have been sadder if we hadn't.' She said it took her seven or eight months before she felt ready to embark on a sexual relationship with another man.

For both Jenny and Douglas, the ability to understand grief was a prerequisite in choosing another partner and forming a new relationship. They could not imagine being intimate with someone who had not experienced and paid attention to a loss of their own, and even then it was not easy. Jenny explains how she coped with a new partner: 'I felt I was not interested in forming a relationship with anyone else. I was still very bound up in myself. Very selfish, I think. But he was very keen on me, and very gentle and considerate and he understood that I had a problem. He understood that there was this man that I had not let go of, who had meant everything to me, and when the subject of sex came up I could *talk* about it, but I couldn't cope with doing it.' She laughed at this point and continues: 'We slept together for about six weeks before I could cope with sex and I was very lucky at that time that that man was willing to wait, and let me say when I was ready.' Before her partner died she had heard it said that people who lose children can make love within hours: 'It did surprise me at the time. I can recall being really startled by that.'

This was something people who had lost children spoke of. For one couple, who had lost a child of thirteen in an accident as she came home from school, that was exactly what happened. The wife recalls: 'We ended up making love on the floor in her bedroom, and then we both just cried our hearts out. We just sobbed and sobbed. I can't explain why we needed to do it, but it was right that it happened. I don't regret it or anything. I think it was a way of being close.'

A father in his forties revealed that following the death of their small child he and his wife also made love: 'It was a way of getting comfort. And even though my wife was on the pill at the time, I think perhaps at the back of my mind was the thought that she might get pregnant. You know, it sounds terrible, because you could never replace a child, but maybe I was thinking it was a way of trying to bring another child into the world because you'd lost one.'

That thought is not, in fact, either terrible or unusual. A psychotherapist says of sex and grief: 'With people who've lost young children there can be an instinct to replace that loss through love-making and possible pregnancy. Sexuality is also used as a release for unbearable tension, whether anger or frustration, and it is often therefore a focus for things that can't be borne, like grief. Loss of libido would be just as common, if not more so, as the wish to have sex. Very often after a death or a shock one partner or the other finds they completely switch off from sex, and that is something that often has to be worked through or coped with.'

The problem of one partner wanting sex and the other not is made considerably worse by an immense loss and the grief and tension this produces, as a couple in their early fifties who lost a son three years ago found. It was the wife who brought up the subject of sex in describing the range of emotions she experienced following her son's death: 'I think the worst thing was . . . we've got a big bed, and we used to go to bed at night and A. [her husband] would sleep on his edge of the bed, and we couldn't get close to each other because we didn't want to upset each other. I felt that if I cried and he heard me, it would only upset him, and he used to think he would upset me. So, although we love each other, that love was such that we didn't want to upset each other more than we were upset already. It was like bouncing a ball between you, this terrible grief, so in bed you'd squeeze as far away from each other as you could.' This lasted for the greater part of a year, and during that time on the few occasions when they had tried to make love it had not seemed right for some reason. While their sex life then returned to normal, she explained that for that first year even the comfort of holding her husband was not the comfort she most wanted, for what she most wanted was the return of her lost son.

Her husband said: 'From what I've read, it is the case that the man wants sex afterwards for comfort, to reaffirm closeness and togetherness. There's a longing for that closeness. And the woman doesn't want this in the same way. Sex to her seems bad in such circumstances. It sounds insensitive from a man's point of view to say you want to make love, but you do, but you don't want to do this against your partner's wishes.

'It's not good unless you respect her wishes too. So for a while it's a bit difficult and I think lots of marriages break up after a bereavement of this kind. I can understand why, because everyone is so wrapped up in their own self-protectiveness. But then there are ways of being close together, and a cuddle and a kiss at the right time is better than trying to have sex before somebody's ready.'

*

There is another unexpected aspect of loss, and that is the fact that it is cumulative. Many people spoke not only of losses coming close together, of there being a series of them, but also of how a second or third grief echoed an earlier one. Within a period of three years one woman in her forties lost three members of her family and her marriage ended: 'Any thought that you could ignore grief, and that it would go away after a while, you know, just disappears into thin air, is dangerous. It doesn't go away, at least not if you ignore it.'

This woman feels that she tried to get on with life too quickly after the first two griefs – her parents dying within eighteen months of each other – and then found all kinds of things conspired to make her take the losses more seriously: 'My flat got flooded from top to bottom, my daughter had an accident at school, all kinds of things kept on happening, and one day I just had to say: "Wait. Hang on a minute. There's something going on here."'

What she thinks was going on was her subconscious telling her she had to recognise her loss more fully than she had done. Particularly, she had to recognise its 'mark' on her: 'Grief does mark you, and I didn't want to be marked. I wanted, in one way, to carry on as if nothing had happened. Something very important *had* happened, and I wasn't going to be able to shake it off. The bit I needed to face was that I had relied heavily on my parents, even though I was a mother myself, and I suppose I was afraid to face the reality that I still needed them when they died.'

Another woman, in her thirties, spoke of what happened to her mother when her mother's parents died: 'My mother was really close to her mum and dad. They lived with us when I was a child, and I thought my mother was taking it rather calmly. She's a woman with strong feelings, but she hardly cried. Then six months after my grandparents died, the dog died. And this is going to sound bizarre, but my mother just collapsed. She rang me up and said: "This is going to sound awful, but I'm hurting more about this dog than I hurt about my mother." I thought it was very brave of her to say that, and I told her it wasn't because she loved the dog more, but because the grief was cumulative.

'I've learned this for myself: if you don't sort out grief when it happens, and give it the proper attention, it gets worse and worse. It's as if life is telling you you have to take notice, and if you don't, you'll keep on getting faced with more loss until finally you wake up one day and say: "I can't carry on like this."'

Where one's own emotions are expressed or resolved, be they tearful, sexual, humorous, there can still be a problem with the rest of the world. Gareth, whose mother died when he was twenty, finds that what has happened since her death is that she has been buried twice: 'I feel names are important to keep someone alive, and yet people are embarrassed to say my mum's name, or to talk about her. Straight after she died my friends would be talking and one of them would say something about parents, and then there'd be a silence. And if people were having a conversation which included parents in general, it suddenly became, oh, you can't mention that because of what's happened to . . . I can understand they were trying to be helpful and not upset me, but my mother was the uppermost thing in my mind at the time.'

Since then he has learned that close friends of all ages fall into two categories, those who will talk about his mother and those who will not. Luckily for him there are a few people in the first category, for he echoed the sentiment of the man discussed in chapter 3 who lost his mother at the age of thirteen: 'I want to remember my mother, and it helps when people talk about her. It's an event I find useful because a lot of my life is moving on without Mum being a part of it. It's important to have that time when my mum was here made real, if you like, because I'm moving away from it. There's already a big part of my life that I've lived without her.'

He also brought up an anomaly about grieving: that it is the mourners, quite often, who help those who are not grieving, and not the other way round. In common with a number of people, he spoke about the fact that there is a kind of person who is attracted to grief, almost in a voyeuristic way, not so much for what they can contribute to ease it, but for what they can get out of it: 'I got annoyed with girlfriends at university who suddenly wanted to spend all their time with me because basically they wanted to mother me. It was a strange thing. I thought I was looking for something to fill the gap in my life. I wanted to talk, and I was a bit lost. But as it turned out I was fulfilling the purpose of sorting out the insecurities in them. Quite a few of my female friends wanted to mother me because it made them feel better. It didn't make me feel better at all.'

When asked if the overtures from his female friends were sexual, he said: 'It's a bit difficult to know what was what, but, yes, I can think of three people – girls – who I possibly fancied before who all of a sudden were really interested in me. In the end the only reason they were interested in me was because they were trying to satisfy something in themselves. I think it was the fact that I was vulnerable. I had the feeling it wasn't *me* they were interested in as myself – and it wouldn't have happened if my mum hadn't died. They weren't interested in me before that, and I had a bit of a feeling of disappointment about it. It ended up being a one-night stand, which wasn't what I was looking for.'

A man who is now in his early thirties and lost his mother ten years ago experienced this too: 'After my mother died, women at work behaved really strangely. They wanted to sleep with me – then nothing else. First of all I thought they were interested in me, and I was pleased. But it wasn't that. They didn't want a relationship, just some kind of experience.' He is now married and has discussed this question with his wife: 'When I first met Kate I was a bit stand-offish, and it took a while before I could trust her. It sounds daft to say it now, but I wanted to know she wanted me for myself and not because my mother had died. I told her what had happened, and with Kate it was different because she wanted me for who I am.' He felt a very bad 'gut reaction' against what he called the 'bad mothering' offered by some women immediately following his mother's death: 'Somehow it wasn't genuine. There was something in it for them, some twisted need, and it felt all wrong to me.'

A bereavement counsellor commented on this: 'I think if you look at any gathering at a funeral, you will find as many hangers-on as you will at a party. They're people with empty lives and they want to be somewhere where something is happening. I can see why they do it. Some funerals are a lot more sustaining and interesting than many parties I've been to. I've attended some wonderful funerals.'

There is undoubtedly a voyeuristic component in people wishing to, as another man in his late fifties put it, 'be part of the action' of grief: 'I noticed it first of all when I was a child. You'd see a funeral procession go by. Those were the days when you stood by the side of the road and waited. And you'd hear certain people standing around asking all kinds of questions about who was so-and-so in the car, had he made up with his daughter, you know, gossipy kinds of things. But more than that, after I lost my first wife some people were round all the time, and I'd see them searching my face as if they were trying to find out something.

'I don't' want you to get the wrong impression. Some people were marvellous, but others . . . There was one woman who was a neighbour, and I thought first of all she was being kind, until I caught her staring at me a number of times . . . It wasn't sexual, but the nearest I can describe it is that she was fascinated . . . She had a kind of ghoulish interest in watching me, and I felt as if she was trying to get, or take, something from me. I began to avoid her like the plague.'

A fascination with people who are mourning was seen by a psychiatric social worker as 'a wish to be "in on" the passion of grief': 'Some people lead incredibly empty lives, lives without passion, and they get, or try to get, their passion from other people. Grief is a very passionate affair. It is a time of extreme emotion. And along with sex, it is a private affair.

'There is a certain kind of person who is fascinated by people who are grieving, as they are fascinated by people's secrets. They want to be part of something as dramatic as a death without having to "do" or suffer any of the grieving themselves. That's why, when you meet these people, you get an uncomfortable feeling. It's because they're expecting you to experience sometimes quite frightening feelings while they sit on the sideline and watch. So they're not sharing, or trying to share, your grief with you, they're just watching it.'

For the person who is grieving, the sense of being watched can feel like a violation. It is somebody else's wish to intrude on a tragedy which they are not prepared to suffer for. It is why theatre, films, TV 'soaps' – and books – play such an important part in allowing people to watch or read about strong emotions like grief through a play or a story. It makes it possible to contemplate passionate feelings from a safe distance, and to experience a little of them at second hand. One of the major attractions of soap operas like *Brookside*, *Coronation Street* or *EastEnders* is that you can watch a character die, contract AIDS or go through the anguish of a relationship breaking up without having to suffer yourself – or feel guilty. Art of all kinds, the work of the great painters, composers and poets, offers us the chance to experience deep emotions.

Music, from opera to popular songs, can also be a focus for getting in touch with emotions which are otherwise difficult to reach. Some people spoke of deliberately putting on a weepy pop song or a beautiful piece of music to make them cry when someone not very close to them had died, but someone they nevertheless cared about. A nineteen-year-old woman said that following the death of her grandmother, music was the key to enabling her to grieve with her father: 'I didn't know her very well. I was closer to my other gran, but she was my father's mother, and for his sake I felt I had to show a bit of feeling. So my dad and I sat in the front room and put on some music and talked about her, and he was crying, and I held his hand and I cried too.'

What one can do for people who are grieving, it seems, is to join them in some way which is sincere, and, occasionally, to risk making mistakes oneself in the process. A woman in her mid-forties whose husband died after twenty-two years of marriage sometimes encountered a 'sitting on the fence' attitude which hurt and angered her: 'Some people didn't phone because they didn't know what to say. Months later they said they felt awkward. But you need them to phone, and you'd prefer them to say the wrong thing than nothing. I needed their awkwardness far more than I needed their silence. There's nothing more "awkward" than your husband/best friend/business partner/father of your children suddenly dying. That's about as awkward as you can get.

'I felt really bereft at one point, having lost so much, and I wanted to scream at people: "Why should *I* be the only person feeling awkward? Why should I have to be such a big loser all by myself?" I really do understand people don't want to make you feel worse by making mistakes or saying something stupid. But really, to be standing up in the world when you've lost the person who meant the world to you feels about as "stupid" as I ever want to feel in my life again. I felt completely exposed, and for other people to have risked exposing themselves a little would have helped a great deal.'

The difficulty people have in responding to those who have suffered loss is one of awkwardness, of not wishing to offend. There is also a fear of facing other people's pain. Partly this is a primitive fear, that if you associate with people who are 'drowning', you may drown yourself; partly it is a wish to get on with the good things in life, which are considered more interesting and pleasurable than loss and death. A combination of these two attitudes can, in fact, produce anger towards a bereaved person. A woman who experienced this after the not uncommon occurrence of having two people close to her die within a few months of each other said: 'You're made to feel careless if you suffer more than one bereavement, as if it's your fault, as if you've fallen foul of the law of averages and there must be something wrong with you. Within a few days of attending the second funeral [of a close friend], I bumped into someone at work who noticed I'd been away the previous Friday. When I told her why, she said: "Goodness me, associating with you is getting to be dangerous." I was shocked, too shocked to reply, and I can only imagine she meant that two people near me had died, so I must be bad news.'

If grief is faced, and all its expected and unexpected components accepted, then it becomes a journey, and for most people a valuable one. Loss is unavoidable – for all of us. People who try to deny this in their own lives and in their treatment of others are, in the words of the cliché, 'storing up trouble'.

* * *

CHAPTER 11

Beginnings within Endings

The misconception that childhood grief does not exist, when in fact grief begins in childhood

One of the worst things we do to people in grief, besides avoiding them as if loss, like the plague, is catching, is to infantilise them. Yet all too commonly we do this – treat people who have suffered loss, or who are in grief, like small children. In part it happens because people who are in mourning often become, for a short while, incapable of doing usual adult things, and it is then easy to take them over.

A woman who is involved in a programme which offers counselling to people who are suffering physical loss, such as the onset of deafness, Alzheimer's, severe arthritis or AIDS, told me at the start of our conversation about infantilising within hospitals: 'We pick this up from patients who go into hospital. People who have been used to being treated like you or me suddenly find they are being treated like children. Someone is asking them to "lift a leg up for me, dear", and it makes them feel awful. It creeps in with people in grief and can have quite a devastating effect.'

She suggested that the reason for infantilising people who have suffered the loss, say, of a partner lies in a wish to distance ourselves from possible tragedies which might befall us: 'If someone else has lost a long-term partner, we fear it may happen to us too. If a neighbour's husband has died, it brings up fears that our husband might be next. By infantilising the neighbour it puts a distance between what's happened to her and what might happen to us. Then we make the neighbour "different" in our minds. And since someone who needs help makes us think of a small child, we think of the neighbour in those terms.'

Many people, following a severe loss, lose their adult veneer for a short time. They become incapable of making small decisions, they might cry uncontrollably and they might, for a few hours, or a few days or weeks, need looking after. People who have accepted the various losses and griefs in their own lives will do this 'looking after' without infantilising. People who are afraid of loss will reject its effects in other people, and either distance themselves or make the people who are mourning different by treating them like small children.

This is a particularly damaging thing to do to a person in grief, for the shock of a severe loss can bring with it more than enough confusion and dysfunction. It can, for example, make usually competent adults temporarily accident-prone. They crash a car, break a leg, drop things, trip up. They can suffer in the way that hurrying – or tired – children can. A woman in her early sixties who was widowed two years ago after forty years of marriage badly scalded her hand within weeks of the death of her husband. She says: 'He would have been so upset – and angry. He always made me take care of my hands.' While she still has the hands of a young woman, the scar is plainly visible; it was made worse by the fact that she did not take care of it. She did not see a doctor until 'it had turned quite nasty'.

A psychotherapist traced the early stages of severe grief, like being accident-prone, back to childhood. She first of all explained the ongoing link between our adult selves and our pasts: 'As adults we become our own "parents". We become capable of looking after ourselves and of taking care of our physical and emotional needs. As children we were looked after. We have learned from that how to take care of ourselves and our own children.

'This can break down for a time in severe grief. We experience overpowering needs and emotions. These can hurtle us back into a state of childlike dependency, and into childish behaviour. So if we can't have what we want, we will throw a tantrum. Grief is in one sense a time of extraordinary frustration, when you want to bang your head against the wall and kick and scream. Instead you find that you've broken a leg, or scalded an arm . . . '

Childhood experiences play a crucial part in grief, for fear and loss begin in infancy. Every infant is completely dependent upon an adult, usually a mother, for her or his well-being. The fear of losing this, and of being separated from the mother, is the first fear. A mother causes the first small grief by removing herself from a baby who still wants more of her. She causes a big grief if she does this often and negligently.

Childhood, in any case, contains all of our first losses: loss of innocence in order to gain knowledge; loss of infantile fantasy in order to understand reality; loss of a child's body in order to gain an adult one; loss, eventually, of being looked after in order to achieve looking after ourselves and, possibly, children of our own. Childhood is a series of leaving things behind in order to move forward to others.

During this process all children cause parents some grief, as parents have, to a greater or smaller degree, aggrieved their children. There is the natural grief caused by growing up and growing away from parents, but quite often there is also deliberately provoked grief. For example, a child who has not got her own way might decide to punish a parent. She might stay out a little longer, or not come in when it is raining, just to make her mother, or father, anxious. A psychotherapist clarified this: 'The child's wish to cause grief is the wish to be loved and cherished turned into anger and aggression towards the parent who seems to be careless of or impervious to the child's wishes. So the child who refuses to eat or who deliberately stays out in the cold wishes to make the parent sorry, to make them grieve. When the child stays out, the motive is: "I'll make them miss me." '

The final – and essential – 'grief' a child causes a parent is to leave him or her. Without this independence is not gained. Tomorrow's adults cannot begin to take charge of their lives and the world around them unless yesterday's parents suffer the grief of the loss of their children's childhoods and, usually, their children's presences in their homes. Where the parents have been strong and wise enough to let this happen, the gains implicit within the loss can be enjoyed. New relationships between parents and grown-up children can be built, and can eventually form the basis of future kindnesses – such as the wish to take care of ageing parents. In other words, the acceptance of essential loss can avert future grief.

This was described by a man in his early fifties: 'All of life is a cycle of life, death and rebirth. I don't know how many times I've "died", through the death of a relationship, of a friend, through my children . . . The cycle goes round and round. There is one sense in which the whole of our life is a mourning, for loss of the womb, of the breast, of innocence. The births and rebirths from all of these are essential to our lives, as they are also nails in our coffins.'

The inextricable nature of life and death, grief and growth and their links to childhood was referred to by a mother in her early forties when she talked of something that had happened to her thirteen-year-old son. He had been set upon and beaten up by a gang of older boys while waiting at a bus-stop one afternoon on his way home from school. He was not badly hurt, but was terribly shocked by the experience of random, senseless violence. He had been brought up to respect people, and to believe he too deserved respect. His mother said: 'I realised he was grief-stricken. He was suffering grief at the loss of his feeling safe in the world. He has known about nasty happenings, but I have tried to show my children the positive things in life, and to protect them a little.

'He lost his childhood that day, and we both grieved. We were both angry, and also aware that things would never be quite the same again.'

Another woman who is a psychotherapist explained her perception of loss: 'Of course we all lose all the time. What affects us adversely is if we lose something before we are ready to lose it. This is particularly so in childhood. I am not sure if one can ever get over the premature loss, for example, of a mother. I have worked with clients who have lost a mother at a very young age, say four or five, and part of me feels the loss to be so unbearable at that age that it produces in the eventual adult an almost bottomless well of grief. I think that's the original grief, loss of the mother. It's there for all of us to some extent, and other griefs are all a derivation of that.'

She spoke of a woman who had lost her mother in her early twenties after a relationship in which they were not close: 'The mother died with her face to the wall. She refused to speak to her daughter, or to acknowledge her presence. Emotionally, she built up a brick wall. Even years later this woman was terribly affected by the manner of her mother's death.'

Loss that is acknowledged seems to act as a release, even if initial acceptance of the full weight of it feels like a ball and chain dragging us down. The psychotherapist said of this: 'People who treat loss seriously know how much of it there is, which is why it can seem overwhelming. What becomes even more overwhelming is trying to avoid it. My job is to help people face their losses, their griefs from childhood, and to accept them. Where this happens you see how the courage of the acceptance brings its own healing and way forward.' As an example of this she cited the women whose mother died with her face to the wall, who has since become a psychotherapist herself – that is, a person concerned with healing others.

A man who works in a child guidance team and is a psychiatrist talked of this potential development as 'finding'. In an attempt to work creatively with the grief of all kinds he encounters in young people he often looks at the positive search, or the energy inside a negative circumstance. He thinks that the grief of people who lacked patents, or adequate parenting, can be viewed not only as losing, but as seeking, or finding: 'As a child – or an adult – you're looking to find something. Most children, for example, are looking for a good relationship with their parents. They want to find this. If you can work with the *quest* of a child in trying to find an absent parental figure, you're working with something positive.'

He went on to say that in working with grief you had first to realise there was a need, and then work out a way of dealing with it, or of fulfilling it. He sees loss and grief, therefore, as potential 'findings' as well as actual losses: the finding, for a child, of a substitute parental figure; the finding, for an adult, of comfort in distress. Her also discussed the syndrome of infantilising people who are in grief: 'If you infantilise someone in grief, you humiliate them by making them believe they are hopeless when they are not. If you allow a person in grief the chance to experience that grief, then you also offer him or her the chance to recover, and to "grow up". In other words, by allowing someone to experience being lost you allow them the ability to find their way out of being lost.'

To look at losing in terms of potential finding allows an accurate understanding of many losses; it also provides some creative opportunities for learning how to deal with loss.

A psychotherapist who specialises in working with children believes it is 'the creative possibility of endings and of accepting change that matter. A child from a stable background will be able to accept the ending of a favourite TV programme or a holiday, for children from stable backgrounds can look forward with optimism to more good things tomorrow.

'How we are brought up is crucial to how we accept loss or endings, and whether we can view them as possible new beginnings. It is the child who has to have the same day played over and over again with the same TV programme, who is clinging to that security and afraid of moving away from it, who causes concern. Children can accept loss if there is something else to look forward to.'

The fact that endings have beginnings within them is commonplace in the natural world. The ending of a day – night – makes it possible for a new day to dawn. The ending of a flower's cycle, when the blossom has died, brings the seedhead for the next flower's growth. An emotional acceptance of this natural phenomenon is, however, more difficult. It is one which causes strain in many families – when a new baby is born, for example. An existing child often mourns the ending of her or his special place, usurped by the new baby.

This happened in a family which was far from being deprived or unstable; nevertheless, the youngest of the three sons would not, at first, let go of yesterday. He would not accept the loss of his 'youngest child status' when his new baby sister was born. He was almost six at that time, so had enjoyed this status for a number of years. He was included in his mother's pregnancy, as was the whole family, and seemed to be looking forward to the new baby. This changed shortly after his sister arrived. The boy, Yves, then found his new sister a direct rival for the kind of attention he was used to having himself. Since it was an open, tolerant family, he made his feelings felt. Arming himself with a feeding bottle, he found some baby books he had grown out of years previously and retired to his old cot. There he staged a sit-in.

At first his parents allowed this and treated it with a mixture of seriousness and good-natured teasing. They were both trained in child welfare, and they decided he should be allowed to display his jealousy. But Yves showed no sign of stopping his protest. He came out for meals and family treats, but spent his 'spare time' in the cot, behaving like a baby. His mother takes up the story: 'After a few weeks he was still in the cot and we began to get worried and phoned up a colleague to talk about it. I mean, how do you judge these things? Is he allowed to be in there two weeks, but not three, or three weeks but not four? Our feeling, though, was that it shouldn't go on for much longer. We wanted him to be allowed his protest, but we also wanted him to know that a protest has to end.'

The colleague's hunch was much along Yves's parents' lines, that Yves was coming to the limit of when his time would be up. A week later his parents delivered this thought to their young son. They told him kindly and firmly that enough was enough. His protest had been duly registered, and he was now required to come out and get on with being almost six in the big bad world outside his babyhood cot. His mother says: 'Things have been fine since then, but I know that it has marked him for life. You can't stop that happening to your children. And the reason I call it a grief, and not just a jealous stage, is because of that mark. He was grieving for his "youngest child" status which he had lost. It was his first major loss in an incredibly sunny childhood, and I felt it was important that we accepted it as such.'

The reason for making a particular point about childhood grief of all kinds is that there is a strange notion that children do not suffer grief. We have the idea that troubles of this kind are only suffered, and also only understood, by adults. Things like death and loss and grieving are supposed to be kept away from children in case they upset them.

This attitude not only denies the reality of millions of children's lives world-wide, those who suffer war, famine, poverty, abuse, neglect, but also denies healthy, well-cared-for children their everyday perceptions, and their abilities. It is clear from listening to children that they talk about death and loss. Small children 'kill' their toys from time to time, or make their babies cry. Even in a loving home their concerns and questions mirror a world of ordinary loss. Sam, the woman counsellor who had a miscarriage and found she needed a surprising amount of time to recover from it (see chapter 8), gave an example of this. She was helped through a game played by a little girl of four or five who lived nearby: 'I was quite close to her and she was thrilled that I was pregnant. She was really looking forward to the idea of sharing in my having this baby. After the miscarriage the little girl's mother told her that there wasn't a baby any more, and the next time she visited me I wasn't quite sure how to talk to her about it because I knew it was a bit of a loss for her as well.'

The child asked her to play a fantasy game, which they often did, building up details and a story as they went along. At some point in the middle of this game the little girl introduced a baby and then said: 'Oh dear, the baby's poorly.' Sam now recalls: 'My mind started whirring and I thought, aha, this could be the fact that she's thinking subconsciously about the baby I've lost. So we carried on with the game where this baby was very poorly and in fact died. We talked about how sad that was, but we also said that because the baby had been so poorly and had to die, perhaps in a way it was all right.'

What then happened was that the child decided they needed to find a way of remembering the baby positively, and she herself suggested, in the story, that they plant a tree where this baby was going to be buried. Sam and the girl 'had this lovely celebration, in the game, of choosing and planting a beautiful tree to remind us of the baby. It was very moving and it just felt so astonishing that she should have the kind of unconscious wisdom of knowing how to handle the whole issue.' Of her own feelings, Sam says: 'I was a bit churned up, but moved that she had brought me something positive from it, and that it was possible for this to be conveyed to me.'

The part grieving plays in the lives of all young people is profound. It stretches from the world-wide to the domestic and the personal. It encompasses the deaths of millions of children through global events like war and famine, and also takes in the deaths of family pets, a parent, a sibling, a teacher or a friend. In a book entitled *Grief* a London-based theatre company called Neti Neti explores the depth and breadth of childhood grief through children's poems and through papers submitted by adults who work with children. The book contains the results of a questionnaire answered by thousands of primary school children, parents, teachers and other concerned adults. The questionnaire listed forty-three topics relating to children's health and well-being. When asked to rate the topics in order of their importance in children's lives and minds, parents considered death to be fortieth on the list while teachers and health care professionals rated it forty-one. Children between nine and ten years of age, however, placed it eleventh.

Recalling the existence, and the intensity, of childhood grief, a woman in her late twenties said she had a vivid memory of herself as a five-year-old becoming overwrought about the (imaginary) death of her parents: 'I remember getting hysterical and going screaming into the garden. "You're not going to die, you're not going to die. I'm not going to let you. I'll take you to a hospital and make you better." I don't remember them being ill at the time, or anything like that. I can't remember what provoked the hysteria about my parents' possible death, but it's obvious that young children know about death.'

Since grief is cumulative, the memory of it from childhood plays a crucial part in deciding how we cope with grief in adulthood. Whether or not we acknowledge childhood loss and how we cope with it will have a large part to play in how we handle loss as adults. A woman in her late thirties recollected the deep yearning she had as a child which came back to her on the death of her husband two years ago: 'The childhood yearning was like the longing for a fairy tale that would last for ever. In a way childhood is a *time* of yearning. You long for so many things that are outside your control, whether it's to be a grown-up or to have Santa Claus come early.'

A few weeks after she lost her husband that feeling came back: 'I had a completely overpowering yearning for him to be back, almost as if I could make it happen if I concentrated hard enough, if I willed it enough. And I found it helped to keep me sane to return to those childhood feelings. Somehow it was important to know that I'd had this feeling before.

'I'm not saying it comforted me. I think I was beyond comfort for a while. But I do want to convey that it kept me sane. I think losing a person you love rocks your foundations so badly that it makes you understand why people can't face it. I was able to face it because I recognised the feeling from my childhood and it must somehow have anchored me.'

The wisdom of acknowledging feelings from childhood as anchors for adult griefs was described by a psychiatric social worker: if we accept and understand grief from childhood, the temporary feelings of need and dependency produced by adult losses will not unnerve us. She also emphasised the importance of accepting the childish component of grief, its throwback to our own childhoods, for contained within this is the power to help or repair loss: 'If we can be compassionate about the full extent of our loss – which is that it has flung us back into a state of dependency – then we will find the time – and the resources – to heal ourselves. For what will happen is that we will be sympathetic, or empathetic, to the hurt child in ourselves, and that in itself will produce in us, almost like a chemical reaction, the forming of the adult resolve to take care of this hurt child. So the *acceptance* of the hurt child will produce a caring, responsible adult who wishes to make the child better.

'You will sometimes hear a small child who is ill or in pain crying to an adult: "Make me better." Sometimes that phrase is "love me better". Not love me in a better way, but use your love to make me better. That is the essence of it. People who are impatient with their grief are impatient with themselves, and haven't learned to care enough for their own needs. People who are patient will in some sense *use* the pain to form the cure.'

Strenuous attempts to avoid this, to turn a blind eye or a resolute back on the 'bad news' of grief, can end up producing, as discussed earlier, the opposite of what is wanted. A powerful example of a case in which grief was not recognised in any way was that of a man, now dead himself, whose wife died of peritonitis on their daughter's fourth birthday. From that day until the day he died of arthritis twenty-one years later he never once mentioned his wife's name. His daughter, who is now in her forties and a mother herself, says: 'He never sent me a birthday card after that day [of her mother's death]. He never recognised the day at all. It was like a curse, and I grew up with that – and without my mother. I don't know if he thought I wouldn't miss her if he didn't talk about her, but he never once spoke her name or anything about her.'

This woman is head teacher of an infants and junior school in a deprived area. She understands the damage her father's actions caused in both of them. At least in her own case she has discovered through it an added empathy with the needs of children. As the psychiatric social worker recommended, she has found within the labyrinth of her own childhood grief a thread which has led her to the heart of grief in other children. She has found, in other words, a beginning within an ending.

She identifies in her pupils the threat of loneliness, of non-acceptance and of alienation as being critical among their concerns. Working in a deprived area, she often comes across children who are lonely and who crave company and the acceptance of other children: 'Children grieve if they are not liked. And this happens to children frequently. Someone will say: "I don't like you."' While this is experienced by the vast majority of children at some time, for some children it persists: 'You always try to watch out for this, for the isolated child. You see the grief clearly on her face. She doesn't understand why this is happening to her, why people don't love her, why she is being rejected. You do everything you can to bring her – or him – back in. You use role-play, stories, plays. You build bridges, you invent games. A child's need to be loved – and the child's grief if this doesn't happen – makes you understand why the abused child will still want to return to the abusive parent. The abuse is seen by the child as a smaller grief than the larger one of being without a real parent at all, of being, in other words, lonely.'

The fact that the beginnings of grief occur in childhood, the place where grief is supposed not to happen, and are so often ignored results in losses for both adults and children. Children are lonely because their real needs and their natural wisdoms are not understood. Adults become inconsolable if their deep-rooted needs are not attended to. A sixteen-year-old boy was aware of the gains to be made from older and younger people respecting and acknowledging each other's losses. He was fourteen when he got the news that someone very important in his life, his godfather, was dying. He was just fifteen when this man, who was only in his early forties, died. The godson, Thomas, visited his godfather for the last time a few weeks before he died.

Thomas felt he owed a great deal to his godfather and, as he and his sister travelled a few hundred miles to visit him that last time, he was deeply concerned about how to tell him that: 'He put so much into my life, the good bits of me, the things that are kind and caring, that I had to let him know this. I had to let him know that he wasn't only an ace bloke who wore great clothes, and was terrific fun and that kind of thing.'

On the long journey to visit his godfather Thom decided he wanted to let him know that he had made 'a big difference' in his short life, and that he, his godson, would not forget it. As the journey's end got closer and closer, however, Thom got more and more nervous. After all, the man he was visiting was dying, and Thom did not want to upset him by being over-emotional. He also knew that once he had said these things, there would be no more to say, that if he expressed them out loud, he would have to accept their finality: 'It's a very final thing to say to somebody. And that's why I didn't want to say it because I wanted to put it off. On the other hand I wanted to get it off my chest.'

Sitting an hour or two later at the hospital bedside, he did say what he felt he had to: 'In the end I just came out with it. I said something like: "There's something I want to say to you." "What's that?" he asks, and I sort of swallowed, gulped and looked down and I said: "I want you to know that out of all the people I've ever known you've made such a big difference to my life." And he looked at me, and I can just see his face, it was just so unreal . . . and that was another thing, I'd never spoken to him like that before. We'd never had that kind of open relationship so much. So for him to hear it must have been a shock.'

Thom then said most of the things he wanted to, but found after a minute or so that he could not carry on: 'I started crying and I just said: "I'm going to miss you so much", and he said: "Ah, come here", and he gave me a big hug and I swear it's the best hug I've ever had off anybody. We just stayed there hugging each other for about a minute. And I could see by his face he was really moved. It had cheered him up because he was so happy about it . . . '

Almost two years after his death Thomas is clear about what he has learned from his godfather and about the enduring legacy of his godfather's gifts to him: 'They're things to do with treating people with respect, and being kind and not being selfish or arrogant . . . And things to do with treating *women* with respect, and how you could be a strong man, like him, and have loads of fun, and be kind as well. He was unique. He had a deep philosophy about life. He seemed to be laid back and non-violent, but he was strong as well. I know part of me is always going to think if I've got a difficult decision on my mind, what would he have done? And I think I'll find a good answer.'

The 'good answer' to the question of where loss and grief begin is that they begin in childhood and in the family. The 'good answer' about the process of grief is to be found here too; beginnings and endings belong in the same home, under the same roof. The family that most loves and sustains us is also the family that will cause us most grief as our parents and those close to us die.

To ignore the inevitable grief within a family, and to deny childhood grief and the capacity of children and young people to mourn, is to stunt our ability to accept grief as adults. It prevents us from finding within our own childhoods the beginning of the ball of thread which will lead us out of grief's maze.

Children's optimism and buoyancy mean that, in good circumstances, they will recover from grief faster than adults – they have more beginnings to find, and more new opportunities to look forward to. The amount of grief we as adults are able to cope with will depend to a large extent on how we view and treat our own and other people's childhood losses. For if we have allowed our childhood griefs, and therefore our ability to recover from them, this will give us a good precedent to work from. It will give us faith in our own abilities and faith in the prospect of new days, new dawns.

* * *

CHAPTER 12

A Plaque on a Rosebush is Not Enough

Difficulties of mourning within a family, and the assistance given by professionals

Given that most people do not live in or have ready access to an extended family, what happens at a time of family loss is that a few people, sometimes only one or two, shoulder a heavy burden. In the past there would have been many people to carry this load, and to help disperse the weight of it. Nowadays the absence of many shoulders makes grieving heavy work for the few. This has made it difficult for individuals to assimilate and 'process' the varied components of mourning. The idea of 'variety' is important, for grief is not a single shade or colour. Our griefs are multi-coloured, with many different textures and levels of intensity.

The absence of a variety of people to help us absorb, reflect – and deflect – our griefs means that we are often left too much alone with them. We fear burdening one or two people with the intensity of our pain and because of this we often end up, in a small family unit, grieving separately.

Separate grieving within a family was discussed by a man in his late twenties whose mother died six years ago: 'My father and I grieved quite separately. For a short while we were like brothers, just afterwards, but that broke down after a few weeks.' It then became clear to him that his father and he were mourning a person who meant very different things to both of them, even though they both loved her and had lived with her. 'He was grieving lots of intimate things which were not part of my relationship with Mum, and I didn't want to know about them after she'd died. I felt it was wrong. And I felt quite awkward about it. As well as that, Dad took it really hard, and

I felt as though I had to take care of him and put my own grief aside. So I started to spend more time with friends. I wanted to be able to grieve losing a mother without feeling I had to put my father first because he'd lost a wife.'

There is a sentimental notion that families 'stick together' during a time of loss, when very often their grieving happens in the manner just described. This man was alone with his father for most of the grieving process. He is an only child and none of the few remaining relatives lives close by, so he did not have cousins, aunts and uncles, great-aunts and uncles and grandparents to help him with his grief. Neither did his father. They both lacked, therefore, the talking, the airing, the stories from the past, the stories from different perspectives that used to make up so much of the talk surrounding a death. They were, in fact, missing perspectives. They were not given the opportunity to view their grief through different people's eyes, and to gain a sense of it 'in the round'. This especially affects children, who can find themselves carrying extra burdens of grief due to there being no friendly aunts or uncles around to dissipate it for them.

A senior social worker who is in charge of a team of volunteers at a large teaching hospice explained how even in a deeply loving family grief can be inadvertently compounded for a child within it. She referred to the deathbed pronouncement 'Look after your mother/father', which she sees as a problem for children: 'They will be told by a dying man or woman: "Look after your mother or your father." It can leave children horribly bound. Things like "you're all she's got now" leave a very strong impression on children. Some live it out.' She cited the example of a family she has known for many years. A younger daughter had taken to heart the words of her dying father that she should look after her mother. Her mother died when the girl was eighteen, but she continued to be dutiful. She has an older brother and sister, and allowed them to grieve first. The social worker says: 'In that family there was a clear hierarchy of grieving that went according to age. Literally, they took turns. The younger sister allowed her elder sister to go first, and then her brother. It was two years after her mother's death before this daughter allowed herself to grieve. Before that, she looked after the others.'

A woman in her mid-forties also spoke of this hierarchy of 'who has lost more' with regard to her feelings of resentment towards her mother after her father died. In the months following her father's death her mother's grief seemed to swamp her own. While she accepted her mother had lost someone she had lived with for the best part of fifty years, as an only daughter she also needed her own grief for a father to be accommodated: 'I tried hard not to feel resentful, but six months after the funeral my mother was still ringing me up whenever she felt low about Dad's death, but she never once asked me how I was feeling, and if I was still upset by it. If she needed to cry on the phone, she did it to me, and yet I was grieving for him too.' Eventually she brought it up with her mother, after seven or eight months had gone by, by saying simply: 'I miss him too, you know.' While she feels there was not a great deal of change as a result of this, she thinks at least her own grief was acknowledged when her mother said on the phone a few weeks later: 'I mustn't forget that daughters miss their fathers as well.'

Another aspect of the problems a family can face in their grieving was described by a counsellor: 'While families do go through grief together, and have that support, they also have the difficulty that they have different needs at different times. These needs don't coincide or coordinate. While one member is angry, another might be feeling very withdrawn, and while one person is coming out of a difficult stage, and mightily relieved to be doing so, another person might be heading for the doldrums. Not only does grief happen in different stages in different people, but it also happens at different times, and for different lengths of time.

'Many families suffer a tremendous amount of stress after a grief, and quite often someone ends up in counselling because of that. Often it's someone in the family who feels their grief hasn't been recognised, or who feels that someone else in the family is grieving in a way they don't like – like being angry, for example. It would be easier if people could be more aware of this. What doesn't help is the message given in the media, on

TV, in films, and in books too, that family support at a time of grief is a wonderful thing. It can be. It can also be illusory, with people feeling guilt and anxiety because the illusion doesn't match painful reality.'

The most painful event in a family, more painful and certainly more prevalent than death, is divorce. Its unenviable consequence can be that every single family member is left to grieve separately and without consolation. It may turn out for the best in the long term, but in the short term it causes a tremendous amount of grief, and often there is very little help available to deal with it.

A man of twenty whose parents separated when he was eight called it 'the biggest grief of my life': 'At least when somebody's died there's nothing you can do about it. When someone's left the house, you torment yourself. You think it's your own fault.

'And the thing is, you think you've left it behind, and you've cried, and that you're going to survive then, but the remnants leave a stigma on you, and years later it all comes boiling up again. You thought you'd sorted it out, but you haven't. I think grief is like a kettle coming to the boil. You think once it's boiled it's over, but it isn't.'

This man has now sought counselling through the university pastoral system and thinks that at last he is 'making sense' of his pain and of his life. Interestingly, he could not accept the help first offered him because he was given a set time each week to go and see a counsellor, and he wanted more than that. He is now able to attend an allotted appointment, but only after the counsellor gave him much freer access to her time for a month or so. He needed first of all to feel that the counsellor was 'sincere' about him: 'I wanted someone to put themselves there for me, not because they were paid to, but because they cared about me as a person. It's rather a strong word to use, but I wanted to be "loved" for myself.'

It has now become much more acceptable for people undergoing separation or divorce to seek some help for themselves, for their children or for both. A counsellor who works with bereavement said: 'Twenty-five years ago when I first started doing this kind of work it was still quite new, and at that time death was what you dealt with. Now I'd say that more than half the people I see are suffering "other griefs", a great many of them through divorce.

'I don't want to give the impression that divorce itself is bad, because it quite often leads to something better all round, but it does cause pain in the short term, especially to children. Really it's a question of people not knowing how to handle it as far as the children are concerned, and one of the tremendous rewards of this work is to see what an important difference help can make.'

In the first instance, hearing things from the child's point of view matters a great deal: 'Just talking to the children, for example, can make a difference. You can't put their world to rights for them, but you can at least allow them to speak. You can find out the shape and the nature of their fears in this situation where their world is falling apart, and you can let them know that you, at least, understand the divorce from *their* point of view.

'The difficulty with divorce is that it is brought about by adults who are usually themselves in grief, and who then have little time and energy to give the children who are, arguably, in even worse grief. What I do with children is to give them the chance of expressing and beginning the long process of coming to terms with something which is, after all, the last thing they wanted.'

Within families that stay together and that look conventional from the outside there are still secrets, many of which do not emerge until a time of grief or crisis. These in themselves create tension and drama and can play a big part in the continuing effect of loss, even when the motive behind the secret is seemingly altruistic. When a woman who is now in her mid-eighties was a small child, the death of one of her cousins was kept from her by her parents and by her older brothers and sisters. She was one of eleven children. At the time of her cousin's death, when she was almost five and the second-youngest in the family, she was told her cousin had 'gone away': 'My mother and father didn't tell me where. But you know as a child when something's wrong, and people were whispering. I knew something was being kept from me, and no one would tell me what it was. I think children understand a lot more than they're given credit for, and I can still say my parents were wrong in not telling me the truth. It would have been better to have cried or been upset than to have gone on thinking for a long time that people were keeping things from me. I remember arguing with my other brothers and sisters, and being upset because they told me I was too small to know certain things.

'I still have some regret about that cousin. I still remember her, and there's a little bit of guilt in me that I didn't mourn her because I didn't know she had died.'

Not knowing about a death would seem to be an unusual event in the high-tech, mass-communication world we now inhabit. So would keeping a death secret. There are, however, secret living 'deaths' – and lives – which tens of thousands of people are involved in through the process of adoption. There are the 'deaths', or lifelong partings, of women who offer their children for adoption, and are often torn by the experience. But modern legislation has meant that these partings sometimes end in the return 'to life' of an adult 'child' many years later. The 1975 Children Act gives adults the legal right to see their original birth certificate, and as a result of this many adult 'children' in their twenties, thirties or forties have sought out their natural mothers. Those natural mothers have often brought up families from whom they have nearly always kept secret the birth of their first-born. Suddenly there is a stranger on the doorstep. This can, in the words of one woman, 'knock families for six': 'I was with my mum one day when she got a phone call [from her first child, a son, given up for adoption] and she went as white as a sheet. I thought Dad had had an accident at work. Then she went into the kitchen. I followed her in and she had her back to me with her head on the counter. I was worried sick. She hadn't said a word by this time. Then she told me . . . '

The Post-Adoption Centre in London offers information, counselling and support. It seems that the process of adoption, which seeks to repair losses – by giving babies to people who are childless, for example – can also create concomitant griefs. Phillida Sawbridge, the Centre's director, made clear why she associated adoption so strongly with grief: 'Grief is all around in adoption. The birth mother has to give up what is usually her first child. The grief for the people who are adopted is that they lost their birth mother, the woman who bore them, and they lost the father. The adoptive parents too are often mourning the child they couldn't have, their own fertility.

'A lot of the work we do with adoptive parents is based on that unresolved grief. Sometimes when you get into the difficulties they're having with the adopted child they go right back to the fact that they have a clear picture of the child they would have had. The child they have adopted is not the child they had in their minds as their child.'

She explained that women who decided, often under pressure, to give their children up for adoption usually spent the rest of their lives denying this event. They formed partnerships, had 'other' children, but kept on finding there were ways in which the first birth returned to them. 'Because so little support or counselling was given, some women then lived with a kind of hollow feeling. They felt a piece of their life had been removed from them, and they mourned it. Then you get all the reminders. If the woman has other children, sometimes the grandparents will be celebrating the child as their first grandchild, and the woman feels dreadful because this brings it all back. And some women describe being over-protective because they are afraid of losing this one, or they are afraid of not being able to relate to the child because they're really grieving for the other one . . . '

She turned to the other grief that is frequently a part of adoption: 'The people who are adopted can't grow up with people they look like. I used to pooh-pooh the whole blood-tie idea, but I can see that you can't dismiss it.' She added that many people who begin the search to find their birth parents do so when they become parents themselves: 'It's all aroused because this baby they've produced is the first blood relative they've ever had.'

Although most of us have a large number of blood relatives, they are often scattered far and wide. And although our world of high-speed travel and high-tech communication is often called 'a global village', it does not provide the daily intimacy we need. A phone call from a relative on the other side of the world does not provide the security and the comfort of a physical presence.

The few physical presences who are around are therefore heavily taxed. It is hardly surprising, given the pressure upon what is often a small family unit and given the demanding nature of grief, that many people need outside help. However, one man, Charles, warned against 'over-professionalising' something as important as grief. He felt certain professionals served him badly and that, had he listened to their advice, he would not have had the funeral he wanted for his wife. Neither would he have had the benefit of certain things after her death which it would have grieved him considerably to be without. The most important of these was that, like David, whose partner Dee was allergic to 'oily' vicars (see chapter 7), he kept his wife's body at home. 'Both the minister at the church and the undertaker advised me against this, and they were totally wrong in that. Absolutely wrong. It was a total mistake on their part. The minister thought it would be too much for me. Thank God I went against his wishes. I had her body at home, and from time to time I, or various relatives, went in to see the body. And I realised how important it was for me to have brought her home.

'I know it sounds primitive, but I didn't want her to enter this maze, which is what the crematorium is, without being home first. I didn't want to send her away to a place she would never come back from without making her safe first. For her to have gone from the hospital to the crematorium would have been like her going from one strange place to another, and I didn't want that to happen to her. I wanted her to go on her last journey from her own home where she was loved.'

He thinks it would have affected him for the rest of his life had he not done this for his wife, and that he would never have recovered from the feeling of regret if he had not stood out for what he knew was right for them both. He therefore explained how important he felt it was for people to take time over a funeral, and not be rushed into decisions that can never be reversed. He said that the professionals dealing with his grief had been wrong in all kind of ways: 'You're always being snowballed by the priests and the professionals into something you don't actually want because it suits them, and it suits their way of dealing with things.' In clarifying this he spoke of how he was told by a large firm of undertakers he went to that he could not have his wife buried on the day he had chosen: 'Thank Heavens I had the sense to "shop around". And it turned out I *could* have her buried on the day I wanted. It's just that the firm I'd been to didn't have enough cars to spare that day.' He ended up going to a small, independent firm of undertakers. 'If you want to know the one most important thing I would say to anyone after a death, it would be, go to independent undertakers who will treat you and your funeral arrangements in an individual way, and who will listen to you.'

A woman in her late thirties also thinks she was badly advised by professionals, but unlike Charles she did not realise this in time to rectify it. For her, the problem lay in the advice she received from all quarters to have her partner cremated, something she and he would anyway have approved of.

Almost a decade later she still pines for a piece of ground where she could visit him: 'It's one of the few things in life I've totally changed my mind about, cremation. Everyone said it was the sensible thing to do, and I went along with it, but I need a piece of ground. I need somewhere I can go and visit, and think, and be peaceful. A plaque on a rosebush is not enough.

'I'm not saying it would have to be for ever. It doesn't have to be for hundreds of years, but for the time throughout the lifetime of those who care for a dead person I think you're entitled to a piece of ground. It needs to be somewhere you can go and be still and thoughtful, somewhere where you can still love that person.'

Most people, however, described professional help of various kinds, especially good counselling, as being of tremendous benefit. In the case of counselling, though, they were keen to distinguish between professional and voluntary help. Many did not find the latter beneficial.

Their complaints touched on the often religious flavour of certain non-professional assistance, something which people found oppressive and unhelpful. They also felt a lack of trust in the abilities of people they saw. A man in his fifties spoke for many when he said, after visiting a local bereavement counselling service: 'I wanted help and guidance, not tea and sympathy. I could have got that at home. I needed someone wise, if you like, someone I felt could put me on the right track. Instead of which I was faced with a person who was kind, but quite unable to answer my questions or understand the deeper level of what I was getting at.'

The role and the extent of professional help available for people coping with loss has increased dramatically in the latter half of this century, for complex reasons. There is the loss of the extended family itself, as well as a greater pressure, as our numbers rise, for individual griefs to be swamped by work and busyness. These unattended griefs then present us with problems which require professional treatment. There are also 'good' reasons. Through knowledge gained this century we have increased out awareness of the crucial importance of understanding emotions, and especially of understanding children and childhood feelings. This has come about through the development of fields like child psychology and psycho-analysis. This knowledge has, in turn, fostered legislation which, when it was introduced in the middle of this century, sought to give all children an education and the right to free health care. People who have been educated and relatively healthy have come to see the importance of understanding and tending inner wounds.

So there is in our present way of living both a tendency to avoid grief because we are busy and, paradoxically, to accept emotions more deeply because we are better educated to believe they are important. The latter has generated a whole umbrella of organisations which help people cope with loss and grief. Many of these have now been reduced in size or closed due to current spending cuts, but, thankfully, a good number still remain. The largest of these is CRUSE Bereavement Care, set up in 1959 to deal with loss and bereavement; it now has 194 branches in Britain. Then there are hundreds of self-help groups and organisations and thousands of professional psychotherapists and counsellors whose work it is to deal with grief of all kinds. Professional therapists and counsellors usually combine working within bodies like hospitals and specialist centres with a private practice.

Family Therapy is one of the professional services available when the whole family unit and its individual members are under severe stress. Its purpose is to allow both individuals and the family group a way of expressing emotions within safe boundaries. At a time of loss or bereavement these emotions can be powerful and contradictory, and the wish not to express them can be as strong as the urge to do so. Emotions within families have long and complicated histories, and many people will not want to speak of them in front of other people in the home.

A father, for example, may not wish to break down and cry in front of an adult son who believes that men do not cry. A daughter may not wish to be vulnerable and expose her feelings in front of a mother she has a difficult relationship with. A mother may not wish to 'hurt' or bewilder a small child by breaking down in front of her or him. She may prefer to try to remain strong and to keep the world 'safe' in her young child's eyes. Yet if there is the death, or loss through separation, of a parent, a child or a sibling, there is also a need to express emotion and to acknowledge grief.

An account of a family which was not coping with its grief was given in an issue of the *Journal of Family Therapy*. It discussed the kind of professional help that was available to a man of forty who phoned his GP to ask for assistance when he was told his wife had only a few days longer to live. The man's wife, who was thirty-seven, was dying of cancer at home, and he and their two teenage sons did not know, in these final days, how to manage.

The GP happened to know a family therapist working in the area and contacted her. She and a male colleague then phoned George, the man who needed help, and said that if he would like them both to visit the home, they would do so. It was explained to George that they found it beneficial to work as a team of two people and that their role in his home would be as guests whom he could ask to leave at any time.

The therapists asked George and the boys about their roles within the family, their feelings and their fears for the future. It became clear that George felt he could not cry in front of his younger son, who was fourteen. But as they all continued to talk, he was better able to express his feelings.

The whole family then sat with Angela, George's wife, who was lying in a bed in the dining room. They were all able, in their own way, to tell her how much she meant to them and how much they would miss her. Angela was able to tell all of her family in turn that she too loved them – and the therapists quietly left. The article concluded by saying that Angela had died the day following the therapists' visit, and that George and the boys had found the visit very valuable.

The reason the visit was needed would seem to have been difficulties in expressing love at a time when if the sincere words 'I love you' were not said soon – and well – it would be too late. This carries echoes of the two women earlier who had both lost parents and who enjoined their friends to form better relationships with their own parents while this was still possible.

As well as professionals of the kind just mentioned, there are the other professionals: the doctors, nurses, teachers, clergy, fire brigade, ambulance workers and police, many of whom cope with other people's grief on a daily basis.

A senior police officer involved in community policing still remembers the day twenty years ago when as a young duty officer he was called to the scene of an accident. As a father was driving his young son home early from his daughter's wedding to put him to bed, he misjudged a bend in the road. When the police officer arrived, the father was sitting in the middle of the road cradling his son: 'The father was crying, and you would have thought the boy was still alive the way he was holding him. He was dead, though. But the man was so distraught I had to sort of pretend the boy still had a chance and I called an ambulance as if he was still alive. They boy was six, the same age as my own son.

'When something like this happens, your involvement doesn't end at the scene of the accident. You have to deal with it all the way through. You meet the whole family and all of their grief head on at the time that it's worst for them. You think you get over it, but that morning I got home after night duty I sat down on the bed and I just broke down. I cried my eyes out.'

In common with many police men and women, this officer has seen hundreds of tragedies in the course of his police work, a good number of which he remembers 'as if they were yesterday'. He recalls another event, also from about twenty years ago, when he was a young officer stationed in a small town on the outskirts of London. There was an underground station almost next to the maternity hospital, and all too frequently a young mother from the hospital would try to commit suicide by throwing herself under a train. The officer says: 'This one particular time, early in the morning, a young woman had succeeded in committing suicide and I had to interview the only witness. She was a middle-aged woman, a really nice person, who was terribly upset by what she'd seen. Later that day there was another "fatal", a motor-cycle accident where two youngsters went into a tree. One of them was killed outright and I went round to his home address to inform his family.' He pauses a moment, and then adds: 'The woman who answered the door was the same woman who had witnessed the accident at the tube a few hours earlier. She was his mother.'

When I asked many professional people how they coped with the large amount of grief they met in a working day and what the rest of us might learn from them, some of their answers were not what I would have expected. I had thought 'the professionals' hardened themselves to grief and became detached, but this is not always the case.

One nurse in her early thirties, for example, was not able to reconcile herself to the death of a young patient until she visited her grave months after she had died. The nurse was off duty the day the girl died, and she was away when the funeral took place, but later she sought out the grave. 'She'd been on my mind for three months and she wouldn't go away. And I realised I had to say my goodbyes to her. So I went to the graveside, by myself, and said goodbye to her properly, in my own way. And I thought about her, and how lovely her hair had been, and how brave and cheerful she had been on the ward.

'And then the sun came out. I felt as if I hadn't seen the sun for months, but as I said goodbye the sun started shining, and I felt better.'

Another nurse, who is now in her mid-fifties, spoke of how fond she became of a patient, a homeless man who, she believed, induced his last coronary almost forty years ago in order to be allowed to stay in hospital. 'You kept them in hospital much longer in those days. He was a lovely man, and all he owned in the world fitted into the small locker beside his bed. He was so happy and pleased to be taken care of and to be fed and warm, and he was unhappy the day before he was due to be discharged to be going back on to the streets again.

'He had another coronary that night, and died, and I felt it was his way of saying he couldn't face the thought of life outside hospital. I cried my eyes out, but my tears were soon cut short by staff nurse who said: "You're not here to turn on the waterworks every time someone dies. You're here to work."'

Even after the death of this man, the nurse, who was eighteen at the time, took care of him, for a less austere member of staff asked her if she would like to 'lay out' the man. After hesitating for a moment, she decided she would because she was the nurse who had been closest to him. 'It was good for me to do it. It helped me. I took enormous care of him. Even with death there's a dignity, and although he was cold, I could still feel the warmth from him within his body, and from the kind of person he was.'

The professionals I spoke with did not talk of hardening themselves against grief as a way of dealing with it. On the contrary, they talked of the importance of understanding what people are going through, and what they themselves gain through this. A bereavement counsellor, when asked what enabled her to take in so much of people's pain, replied that she found her job highly rewarding: 'One major thing is you see people come out of it. People do. Most people do. You see people at their worst, at their most helpless, at their saddest, and then you see them come alive again, and the satisfaction of that is so enormous. You only have to see it a few times to give you hope for all of the others, and for that hope never to leave you.'

Professional people also made clear their own need for support, both in a systemised way through their own institutions and informally through colleagues. The undertaker who was quoted in chapter 10 said that humour was a vital weapon for him and his colleagues in helping them to unwind. He also reinforced the bereavement counsellor's comments about his job being rewarding, for he said he does it because he likes working in the community: 'The amount of community work involved in being a funeral director is surprising. You're meeting people at a time when they've suffered a big loss in their lives, and they tend to rely on you for a while. You get very involved with people, and that's what makes it a wonderful life. There's always people coming round to see you.

'I think helping people after the funeral's over, which is often the time they need it most, is a lot of what this job's about. Someone will come in three weeks after the funeral, and they'll asks you something about some arrangement or other. And you know that's not why they've come. They've come because they want to talk, because they're finding their grief difficult. And you can help them. You can console them without being sympathetic in the wrong way, and you can help them without giving them pity – which is the last thing they need.'

What most appeals to him about his work is that he is able to help people with their grief, and can sleep with a clear conscience at night: 'I can do something to the best of my ability, and at the end of the day I can help the living. For every one dead person we see, we see at least six living. And to be quite honest, our job is not with the person who's died. There's nothing more that can be done for that person. It's what you can do for the living that counts.'

What good professional people do for the living after a bereavement can take all manner of forms. It can range from providing a shoulder to cry on at a time of deep distress to offering long-term counselling or therapy. Almost half the people I interviewed had had some kind of professional help, even if it was just one visit to their GP or one session with a counsellor. About two thirds of these had found the experience useful, and had gone on to seek continuing help, mainly for the purpose of understanding the deeper griefs underlying a present one. Those who felt they had not benefited from counselling had seemed to survive well. The experience would appear to have given them added confidence in their own ability to manage their grief in their own way.

The idea, then, that a family these days should be able to deal with its members' griefs as if 'the family' possessed magical healing powers is not realistic. It is reasonable, and usual, to expect support from a family member, but where grief is concerned it can also be wise to seek healing from other places. For while there is, thankfully, a part of grief which can be shared, which is part of our human community and which is part of what makes us human, there is also a part which is separate and unique, and which we must care for ourselves.

* * *

CHAPTER 13

Not the Only Tragedy

The way griefs are linked, and how the knowledge of this affects our relationships

How we are affected by grief can be extended far beyond the activity of mourning one person who matters to us. There is the fact that the experience of grief is cumulative, one loss informing the next. There is also the fact that once we begin accepting our own griefs, we can empathise with the pain of others. We are then, in turn, able to understand grief itself in a broader way and in a fuller context. This is crucial to our journey through the pain of grief, because if we cannot, eventually, contextualise our loss, we will feel forever victimised. If we think our tragedy is the only one, we will never recover from it. When we understand grief more fully, contrary to our worst fears, we are not usually dragged down by the weight of it. Instead we are guided towards an appreciation of our own loss within a wider spectrum, which stops us being defeated by it.

What grief does is to challenge us. It confronts us with powerful emotions and large questions: questions of justice, of pain, of whether life is random, of whether or not there is a god, of whether or not we matter and, if so, how. It also presents us with the fact that it is hard for adults who are used to imposing order on their lives to come to terms with the often random or accidental nature of a loss. It can be difficult to accept that there is nothing we can do to retrieve what has gone. 'Surely there must be something we can do?' we ask. 'Surely there must be someone or something we can turn to?' What one is presented with, in these questions, is a journey towards finding some kind of answers. However, it is a journey we undertake unwillingly;

we come to it with reluctance, and bearing our losses heavily. As well as loss of a person, there are all the other losses which a parting brings about: loss of safety, security, intimacy; and loss of an idea, the youthful idea that our power is absolute, and that we can carve ourselves a safe niche where loss, abandonment and death will not reach us.

When they find us out, it is hardly surprising that we try to defend ourselves. We attempt to make ourselves less prone to the accidental nature of life by trying to impose some kind of order. For if life were this arbitrary all the time, if people we cared for were just removed from us at whim, it would be unsustainable. It would be impossible to build relationships in such an atmosphere.

The way we climb out of this chaos is, first of all, to accept that we are in it, and that a personal tragedy, usually not of our making or our choosing, has occurred. If we take the journey, instead of denying or rejecting it, then what we discover along the way is that what begins as a narrow, frightening path gradually broadens out. We find that ours is not the only tragedy, and we discover this in our own way. We discover the link between our individual tragedy and other people's grief.

We do not come upon this link via the admonishing tones of clichés like 'There are other people worse off than you, you know.' Instead, we discover other people's grief as we have found our own, through allowing ourselves to accept what is already there, the reality of loss.

When we accept that ours is not the only tragedy, and that we are not the only people ever to have been hurt, we find within ourselves compassion for others, which is a vital part of our own healing. But we cannot properly utilise this feeling for other people without first of all discovering its source, and that is compassion for ourselves. If we have not begun the journey of understanding grief prompted by a concern for our own sorrow, the help we give others is less useful than it might be and we cannot further help ourselves. Self-discovery has to come before concern for others, and needs to be accepted in this sequence when dealing with other people.

A woman called Fay who suffered a miscarriage described how she felt cheated by what she considered to be a wrong sequence of events. She suddenly discovered, through grieving for her own loss, that many other women she knew had been through a similar experience to her own. But they did not tell her about it until she herself was grieving, which was not the right time for her: 'When you have just suffered grief, you want to talk about the uniqueness of your own experience. That's what matters. This is happening to *you*, not to anyone else, and the last thing you want is for someone to say they know how you feel because it's happened to them too.'

The two stages then became clear to her: at first you need other people to comfort you 'as if you're the only person in the world this has happened to'; only after that do you want the comfort of knowing you are not the only person who has ever dealt with it. 'I felt accosted by people telling me of their experiences of miscarriage when I was going through my own grief over it. Especially when I was hearing this for the first time. Why hadn't they told me before?'

Fay thinks that what would have benefited her most would have been to have known something about grief in general beforehand: 'When it happened to me, I felt as if I was the only person in the world who didn't know anything about grief, a bit like a conspiracy, as if grief was a club I hadn't been allowed into.

'I would have liked the opportunity to have thought about it before it happened to me. Then perhaps it wouldn't have been quite such a shock. It's part of the way our society doesn't cope very well with death and loss that it's something we don't talk about. And it was like a whole area of truth that was concealed from me, and is concealed from everybody – until it happens to you.'

With regard to what she would like to see changed about this, Fay says: 'I think we know about grief from when we're children, and instead of having it swept under the carpet, I think it should be talked about in schools and homes. Then it would become part of our general experience.

'It should be part of a wealth of experience that is passed on generationally, as we pass on our other human experiences. Then we would have the chance to learn what to do with it. What I've learned is that it's vital for us to be allowed to have the truth of *our own griefs*. When we have that, we can then empathise with other people and allow them to empathise with us. But if we don't have general information to begin with, all this easily gets confused and jumbled up.'

The shape of an individual grief is both unique and shared by other people. It is dependent upon the nature of an individual relationship and shares much with all other relationships. The ability to accept grief and to find things in life which are sustaining, and worth living for, depends to a large extent on being able to link these two ideas.

Were we not able, eventually, to share our griefs, and to understand that others too have grieved as painfully as we have, we would be completely lost in our pain. We would be without direction or perspective, and would feel isolated. We would consider ourselves victimised by our misfortune, and would not be able to draw on the comfort of those who tell us they understand how we feel. We would also be unable to give comfort, and to benefit from doing that. We would, in essence, be unable to receive and give love.

In order to gain comfort through grieving and in order to give back that comfort to others in turn, it is clear there must be a certain sequence in grief: one has to have one's own loss recognised by others as unequivocally unique before one can go on to draw comfort from the fact that in some sense it is not. We recognise that while no one else has lost our husband, our wife, our child, they have lost their own. This common experience is what we can then share with them, which is what turns our individual, lonely grief into a burden which can be at least partly eased. For this to happen, though, the sequence of events has to occur in the right order. The journey of grief has to be acknowledged as our own and undertaken as such before the path broadens to accommodate the suffering of others.

In the shape of mourning, in how it occurs and how it is recovered from, age is another factor which can determine events. Many older people interviewed said that losing a partner after forty, fifty or sixty years together usually had a different set of consequences from those after losing a partner when you are younger. Younger people have more hope and prospect of finding another intimate relationship, or of making big changes in their lives. For some older people left behind, not only could life never be the same, but it stopped altogether. A few people gave instances of friends in their seventies, eighties or nineties who simply 'faded away' after the death of a partner.

This is not to suggest this happens frequently or as a matter of course. Some older people had remarried, some found sustenance in continuing work, in involving themselves in the community, in grandchildren and in 'making the best of things'. Perhaps the feelings of people who had lost relationships lasting many decades are best summed up by a woman in her late sixties. She had lost a husband, and wrote to a friend who had just lost hers: 'It will get better, be assured of that. But it will never be well.'

The fears expressed by people interviewed for this book fell loosely into two categories, one internal, or private, the other external and connected with customs and usual practice. The internal one is a fear, in its initial stages, about the duration of grief. Will it last for ever? Will we ever be free of it? And if it continues much longer, will we go mad?

The external fear is to do with conventions. There is much fear and inhibition surrounding what is 'normal' in grief, a fear of failing to do what is seen to be right, of being different from other people. Is it 'right' or 'wrong' to view a dead body? Do you hold a dead person, and kiss them, or is that 'wrong'? Does smelling somebody's clothes the day after they die make you socially, and emotionally, suspect? Is making love hours after the death of a child shameful?

The purpose of this book has been to suggest that the answers to these and to any other questions about grief lie within individual people's grasp, and are individual decisions. For example, two quite different accounts from the many given show how strongly the decisions we make about the display and custom of our griefs belong to us, and are different, as we are. One is the story of David, the man who would not let the body of his dead partner be put in a mortuary fridge. He was deeply comforted by keeping her at home. The other is that of the woman whose father died and who was terrified during the following nights that his 'marble figure' would harm her. Although she is pleased now that she went to see her father's body in the mortuary, it was nevertheless something which frightened her.

The answer, therefore, to the question of whether or not you view the body, whether or not you touch it, depends on whether or not you wish or need to do that. Barring religious conviction, there is no right or wrong attached to it in itself. Neither is there any right or wrong to love-making after the death of a child, to desiring objects for a while – or to giving away these objects when the time is right.

Of the inner conflict during grief, a bereavement counsellor said fear of madness caused by intense emotions was the biggest fear she encountered among people she saw: '"I'm frightened of losing my mind" is something I hear so often. It happens, especially, where the identity of the person remaining was heavily dependent on the person who has gone. And in that sense it's understandable.'

She backed up what the psychiatrist in chapter 11 said about 'findings': 'It's not that they're going to lose their mind, but they have to *find* it. Their "mind" – or should I say their identity – is so much in the person who's dead and gone that they don't know who they are without that person. So they have to *find* themselves. This is what I try to show them, that they do have skills, competences and an identity which is their own.' It is for this reason that people who are independent in a relationship, and who are young enough, cope better with loss. They are able to work with its consequences – change – with a degree of confidence in their own abilities. They do not believe their abilities have been buried within a dead person, or have fled with a departed one.

Fear of madness was a fear I myself came across in people I interviewed. In essence it is the fear that the grief would last for ever, that its desolation would never lift. This was felt by a man is his early fifties when his wife left him: 'I thought I would go out of my mind with grief. I think it took me about eighteen months to feel safe again, to feel that the ground would stay solid beneath me, that I myself was solid. Before that I went through indescribable feelings. The nearest I can come to explaining them at all is to say that *I* wasn't in control of them, and I don't know who was. I think it was a case of the feelings ruling me rather than me ruling the feelings.'

After hearing a number of people talk of their fear of being overpowered by their emotions, I began to get a sense of the hidden reverberations in the phrase 'going out of your mind', or at least in the fear of this happening. I wondered if, in principle at least, the fear among usually stable people of losing their minds could be turned round and viewed slightly differently. Instead of trying to reassure people that experiencing grief need not make them lose their minds, it might be useful to explore why they wished to leave them. For there is a wish to close down, to leave, or to absent oneself from one's own powerful pain. The wish is actually there. It is not, however, a wish to leave or to step out of our minds, but a yearning to be free of the pain of our emotions. The fear is not one of madness, but of acceptance. It is a fear about finding – or facing up to – painful emotions that we think we will not be able to bear.

If we look at it this way, we need not fear for the safety or sanity of our minds, but could look instead to the blaze of our emotions. It is these which cause so much pain in us, as they should and must do for a while if we loved the person we lost. Pain is an inevitable response to the loss of love. If we understood this too, that our emotions are appropriate, and that our minds are safe and competent to bring them eventually to some kind of tolerable level, we would manage. We would find within ourselves, and with the help of others, a way of cooling the rage and fire of our feelings.

The phrase 'find within ourselves' is extremely important in the facing of loss, for a big fear in grief is that it will never end, and the world will never look bright or hopeful again. To overcome this, a beginning has to be discovered within an ending. Like old fires which nomadic people used to douse to one small spark, and then rekindle, the new fire is lit from the old.

While the shapes of grief are completely individual to those who suffer them, they also carry generally recognisable shapes as well. When speaking of the different shapes of grief, by far the majority of people gave a description of something which went in and out, like a tide or like the shape waves made at the tide's edge. Grief and its attendants seemed a long way away sometimes. Then suddenly feelings came crashing back in again. A few griefs, though not many, went almost in a straight line, from despair out to hope again.

Another 'shape' attributed to grief was a round one, where emotions came round, like rides at a fairground. Sometimes anger, say, had swirled away, and then there it was, back again on the carousel, taking you with it. A woman who had had what a psychoanalyst called 'an unfair distribution of grief' in losing both of her parents, her sister and her marriage within a short space of time said that for her, emergence from grief was like getting off a bumper-car ride: 'After about two years I was feeling less fragile, I suppose, and I started to get on with my life. I was tired of grief. I'd had enough of it.' She described how, shortly afterwards, she experienced a different reaction to the people who had died: 'I became very strongly aware that they'd had their "go". It was finished for them, but I was still alive. My "go" was still going on. And I thought, it's my turn now. I thought of it as like bumper cars. They'd got off the ride, and they'd had their bumps, and their bashes and their highs and lows. Mine – and I felt this in quite a selfish way – were still to come. I still had some rides left. And I felt really strongly that I mustn't let my ride be spoiled by harking back to the past all the time.

'I felt quite determined about this. In my mind I was saying, although the things that are ahead of me are things I can't share with them, it doesn't mean to say that they're not worth having or doing.'

What emerges only after the acceptance of grief is the opportunity for getting back on the bumper car and seeing where it takes us. There is the opportunity for learning, for gaining new ground and for finding new abilities within ourselves. Stephen was in his early forties when he and his wife received the news that she had incurable cancer and had less than a year to live. It was then that he found within himself strengths, insights and abilities he did not know he was capable of. While he and his wife had time to prepare for her dying, as she came closer to death there were decisions to be made of a kind that Stephen had not faced before. He found the ability not only to cope, but to treasure the last few weeks of his wife's life: 'By the time she died I was ready for her to go and I was quite calm. It was eleven o'clock in the morning. I called the doctor, and then I went back to her and held her and cuddled her. I was just alone with her crying constantly, and then, eventually, these things do stop, I got up and got on with what had to be done.'

Stephen said that before his wife died he would not have had the confidence to arrange a funeral in the way he did since she was the stronger and the more capable of the pair of them. Neither would he have had the 'courage' to face a dead body, for this is something he was previously slightly frightened of. Now, however, 'that's gone. It must have started to go when she got seriously ill and I began to nurse her, to clean her and to care for her. And I've learned from that the link between birth and death. I cared for her and I cradled her as I cradled my children when they were born, and cared for them as babies. And having witnessed death *so* closely, having seen, on that last morning, how her breathing was very deep, and how at the end of one out-breath there wasn't an intake of breath to follow, I've come to the conclusion that birth and death are a mirror image of each other. That's what I've learned, and it's made me less afraid of dying – and of living.'

Stephen believes that it is still more difficult for men to grieve and to show their grief, but that this is improving: 'People come to grief and to dying so unprepared, and I think within this it's less acceptable for men to grieve anyway. But I think the more men become involved with the birth of their children, and in their upbringing, the more they will learn not to be afraid of emotions, and not to be afraid of grief.'

During the course of researching this book, the other idea which began to emerge, besides the shape of individual griefs and the discovery of the threads linking one grief to another, is what emotional duty we owe the dying. Both professionals and bereaved people had noticed a problem in our relationship with the dying. As people find it difficult to let go of relationships where someone has left them, so they find it difficult to let go of someone they know is going to die. It was a woman who is now in her forties, and whose mother died twelve years ago, who first spoke about this. Her mother had had 'a massive stroke', yet she needed her mother to recover. Her mother would have been content to die at that point, but her daughter was not ready to let her. She still needed her: 'We managed to keep her alive for thirteen months. The doctors were amazed, but I couldn't bear her to die. She was my best friend, the person I always turned to when I needed advice, so we nursed her better. We brought her home and cared for her. The doctors were amazed at that too. Thankfully, she didn't lose her speech, but she was paralysed down her left side.'

In those last thirteen months of her mother's life they went for car-rides together and talked to each other. They talked about the mother's fears of death as well as her daughter's, and finally they both felt they had had the time they needed. 'In the end I remember we had one long conversation in the car and I more or less said to her: "It's OK now. I'm strong enough. You can die if you want to, and maybe this is no life for you anyway. But if you go now, I'll be all right, I promise you." ' The mother died within three months.

A woman who counsels people at a hospice described a tendency among people to want to 'hold on' to the dying instead of allowing the person to die in their own time: 'Very often it's because the right words haven't been said.' When asked what these right words were, she replied: 'Most of my work with people beside the bedside is moving them towards the words "I love you". For one of the problems for the dying is that people can't say those three simple words. I try to move people towards being able to say: "I love you, and I'm going to let you go." '

Perhaps a hidden reason, besides unsaid words, for not letting go of people is that once this happens, grief must begin. It is possible with a living person who has left us to entertain the thought of their return, and while a dying person is still alive, then so is hope. And perhaps the most frightening thing about grief is that for a short time it obliterates hope. It also, for a short time, makes it difficult to draw comfort from other living people. If someone has died, one's life is so much still with that person, and not among other living people.

When talking about not letting go and the difficulty for a while of relating to the living, not the dead, a number of people mentioned the film *Truly, Madly, Deeply*, made by Anthony Minghella. It features Juliet Stevenson as a woman whose lover, played by Alan Rickman, has died. She cannot get over his death, and cannot draw real comfort from people around her. Holes start appearing in her flat, rats start appearing in the holes and huge holes start appearing in her life.

After this has gone on for some time her ex-lover comes back to her – as a rather unusual ghost who, although he is not alive, is nevertheless flesh and blood. Unfortunately, he does not come back alone, for after he died he made a number of friends in wherever it is that ghosts congregate, and they come with him. They spend their time lying around the flat watching television. This is when life really gets tough, for the heroine finds out that living with the dead is much more difficult than living with the living.

The full message of this film can take more than one watching of it – and copious supplies of tissues – to appreciate. 'Are you telling me there are dead people in my living room watching videos?' is one of the funnier lines. But our heroine eventually grows resentful of these dead people who are crowding in on her life. She becomes angry that every time she wants to spend a quiet hour in front of the television she has to ask a pack of complaining ghosts to switch off *Terminator 2* on the video.

As well as bringing a breath of fresh, honest air to an area which has had far too little, the film highlights the fact that the living must, in the end, live with the living, as those who have lost relationships must live with the prospect and reality of new ones, and not the ghosts of the old ones. If they cannot, or will not do this, their lives are not creative, their days are not lived and dead relationships from the past block off new relationships in the future.

The shape of individual grief is unique. Paradoxically, the more that is appreciated, the more it is possible to see the similarities in all grieving, and to feel compassion for other people's losses as well as our own. It seems the more we understand, accept and express our own feelings, the more we can do this for others too, and the more they in turn are empowered to help us, and we to help ourselves.

This is the fulfilling nature of grief, that it should lead, drive or impel us past our usual daily boundaries to mend the hurt in ourselves and to change the hurt in others. But before helping anyone else, we have to know ourselves. We have to have had the patience to care for our own griefs, to have undertaken our own journeys, otherwise we are only sightseers or tourists along the path of grief. If we neglect the opportunity of making our own journey, then we neglect ourselves and others. We cast aside the opportunity to find a new beginning.

In the end, the creativity, possessed by all of us, is the ability to create from time, and through other people, something which matters. We do this as individuals, for our uniqueness is what is loved and prized in us, and is therefore what is missed when we die or leave.

We are loved for who we are – our individual selves. If we were all the same, our personal searches for meaning and our struggles for relationships which matter to us would not occur. Love as we know it would have no place in our lives, for our love for someone, whether a child, lover, sibling or parent, depends on our recognition of them as individuals. Religion or religious thought would have no place in its present form either, for all religion is based on the idea of individual accountability.

This sense of individual accountability works at its best when a deep sense of communion or 'society' with other people is also felt, for without the latter we could not share, recognise and help each other with our hopes, our loves – or our griefs. We and our griefs, and the griefs of others, are indeed intertwined.

The reason for writing a book of this kind in this way has been to air fears, to make public certain aspects of loss or grieving which people felt were hidden or denied, and to give shape and voice to individual grief. The wish behind this has not been to isolate the bereaved, but, on the contrary, to demonstrate how individual griefs need to be understood in a wider context.

Mourning the death or the loss of one individual is an act of recognition of our human need for relationship: for company and comfort. It says that one person matters to another because of who she or he is, and that no one else can matter in exactly the same way because they are not the same person. Whether or not we matter depends on the content of our hearts, and that 'mattering' is called 'love'. If we label it 'love' or 'affection', it comes from the same source – our wish to relate closely to other people.

Those with contented, peaceful hearts can do this more fully than others. And this is grief's most profound creative gift, the possibility of loving more deeply.

* * *

Afterword

It can be argued that a reader has a right to know an author's motivation in writing any book, especially one dealing with a subject like this. Mindful of that, I would like to explain this book's genesis, and why the word 'good' simply had to be in its title.

In 1985 my first cousin was killed in an accident. She was delivering parcels on foot for a part-time job when she was struck by a car. Since she and I were partly brought up together as children, and since she was a lovely woman with a calm nature and a gift for friendship, I was deeply hurt by her death, as was the rest of the family.

When I travelled to Cardiff to join them the following day, my aunt and uncle were in shock and despair from losing their only daughter at the age of thirty-two. My aunt took hold of my arm the moment she saw me, and when I retrieved it for my own exclusive use about a week later, it was heavily bruised from her leaning on it.

Two days after I arrived my uncle took me aside and asked if I would do something for him. My heart filled with dread when he told me what it was. He wanted me to go to the police station to find out the name of the man who was driving the car that had killed his daughter. He then wanted me to visit this man to learn what kind of person he was and to report back my findings.

In any other circumstances I would have refused, or at least argued, but grief confers on people a dignity and also a persuasion. I felt trapped, as in the gaze of the Ancient

Mariner, and indeed my uncle had just retired from a thirty-year career in the Navy. I did not feel I had the power to cross or thwart him.

As I was leaving the house, I was further dismayed to find my aunt at her accustomed station – holding on to my arm. I suggested she should not come with me, but she exerted a power over me that was equal, in its own way, to my uncle's. She managed to look both deeply wounded and completely adamant at the same time. So we left the house together.

To my surprise the woman police officer at the desk at the police station gave us the driver's name and address; the man lived only a ten-minute walk away. I had thought the police might fear reprisals in cases like these, but apparently we had a legal right to the information. Before letting us go, the police officer told us that the car had been thoroughly checked after the accident, and was completely in order; its brakes, tyres and lights were all in good condition, and all properly working. She repeated what we had already been told, that it would appear my cousin had stepped on to the road without looking, and the driver had no chance of avoiding her.

Fifteen minutes later we were sitting with this driver in the small flat where he, his wife and two teenage daughters lived. He had answered the door to us, and he looked so gaunt and anguished that I had wanted straight away to flee rather than give him any more pain. When I told him, hesitantly, who we were, he at first moved to close the door, and it was only when I said something like 'We haven't come to hurt you' that he let us in. What followed in the next hour is one of the most remarkable experiences I shall ever have. The whole family, father, mother and two daughters, were in a terrible state of suffering, which they began to tell us about. The man had not slept in three days or nights, and his wife explained how in almost twenty years of marriage she had never seen him cry before, let alone weep unceasingly.

As the three of us sat on the settee, I in the middle, my aunt on one side of me and the man on the other, my aunt took his hand in hers and told him through her tears how much she hoped he would soon be better.

It is probably best not to write down all that was said. The family tentatively expressed their need to attend my cousin's funeral, to pay their respects, and my aunt unequivocally agreed. She told them they would be made very welcome, and that she would like them to come.

Just before we left, my aunt fumbled in her handbag for something. She eventually brought out a small bottle containing a dozen or so tablets which the doctor had given her to try to help her sleep. Carefully she counted them out on to the sideboard and split them into two halves. She then picked up one half, and gave it to the car driver. 'Please have these,' she said. 'I hope they help you to get some rest. You need it, and you deserve it.'

When we returned to my cousin's flat, my uncle was sitting in exactly the same place as when we had left him, and that in itself spoke volumes. He is usually a very active man, having spent three decades in an active career. But he was sitting as he had been two hours earlier, in an armchair in a corner of the living room, hiding behind a newspaper. The newspaper was probably turned to the same page.

'Well,' he said, looking up with what I now realise was tremendous caution in his eyes. For if the man we had visited had been an uncaring person, my uncle would have needed some kind of justice. He would have needed to settle a score in some way, even if only by going round and telling the man exactly what it felt like to lose a daughter.

It was relief, therefore, that flooded through him when I said, 'He's a decent man, and he's as upset as we are.'

My uncle got out his handkerchief, as his father before him – my grandfather – had always done at a time of emotional stress. He wiped away the tears, blew his nose and carefully put the handkerchief back in his pocket again.

'Well,' he said, in a broad Welsh accent, 'that's it, then. If he's a decent man, there's no more to be said.'

There are, in fact, just a few more words to be said. First, I wish to acknowledge the debt this book owes to the man whose car killed my cousin, and to his family. Had they been uncaring people, it might not have been possible to write it in this manner.

It might not, in fact, have been possible to write it at all. Secondly, the book's title, which, once it arrived in my mind, refused to leave, is indebted to my aunt and uncle, and especially to my aunt, whose goodness it draws on. It is to her daughter, Linda, that *Good Grief* is dedicated.